# Trapped

I Talk You Talk Press

Copyright © 2019 I Talk You Talk Press

ISBN: 978-4-909733-31-3

www.italkyoutalk.com

info@italkyoutalk.com

All rights reserved. No part of this publication may be resold, reproduced, stored in retrieval system, copied in any form or by any means, electronic, mechanical, photocopying, recording or otherwise transmitted without the prior written permission from the publisher. You must not circulate this publication in any format, online or otherwise.

This is a work of fiction. Names, characters, businesses, organizations, products, places, events and incidents are either the products of the author's imagination or are used in a fictitious manner. We have no affiliation with any existing companies mentioned in this story. Any resemblance to actual persons, living or dead, existing stories or actual events is purely coincidental.

Although the author and publisher have made every effort to ensure that the contents of this book were correct at press time, the author and publisher do not assume and hereby disclaim any liability to any party for any loss, damage, or disruption caused by errors or omissions, whether such errors or omissions result from negligence, accident, or any other cause.

For more information, see the Copyright Notice on our website.

Cover illustration image copyright: © Nejron Photo #31962500 Adobe Stock Standard Licence

# CONTENTS

| | |
|---|---|
| Places and Characters | 1 |
| 1. Blair House | 3 |
| 2. The guests | 6 |
| 3. Chris goes to the city | 10 |
| 4. A change in the weather | 14 |
| 5. No phone, no Internet | 17 |
| 6. A party | 21 |
| 7. Horror in the morning | 24 |
| 8. Max in charge | 28 |
| 9. More bad news | 32 |
| 10. The ride | 36 |
| 11. More questions than answers | 39 |
| 12. Tell me about the guests | 42 |

| | |
|---|---|
| 13. Ginny's story | 46 |
| 14. Elsa's story | 49 |
| 15. I saw a boat | 52 |
| 16. A face at the window | 56 |
| 17. Chris's story | 58 |
| 18. Max's ideas | 62 |
| 19. Life matters | 64 |
| 20. I am alone | 67 |
| 21. Poor Ginny | 71 |
| 22. Where are you going? | 74 |
| 23. A year later | 76 |
| Thank You | 77 |
| About the Author | 78 |

# PLACES AND CHARACTERS

*Blair House* – a private hotel on a remote part of the coast
*Walford* - a fictitious small town 20km from Blair House
*Lockton* – a fictitious town - 50km from Blair House
*Auckland* – a major New Zealand city
*Blairglen River* – the river between Blair House and Walford.
*Stella Olsen* – wife of Chris Olsen. Chris and Stella own and run Blair House Hotel.
*Chris Olsen* – husband of Stella. Chris and Stella own and run Blair House Hotel.
*Jake Olsen* – Chris's brother.
*Lou Cottingville* – a guest who arrives with his wife to stay at Blair House.
*Elsa Cottingville* - a guest who arrives with her husband to stay at Blair House.
*Ginny* – an American woman. She is a keen birdwatcher. She is staying with her friend, Amy, at Blair House.
*Amy* - an American woman. She is staying at Blair House with her friend Ginny.
*Wayne* – a guest at Blair House Hotel. He is staying there with his wife, Angela and his daughter, Chantelle. Wayne says he likes fishing.
*Angela* – a guest at Blair House. She is staying there with her husband, Wayne and her daughter Chantelle. Angela likes television.
*Chantelle* – a teenager. She is staying at Blair House with Wayne and Angela.
*Delia and Gilbert* – a middle-aged couple staying at Blair House Hotel. They like eating.

*Max* – an older man who is staying at Blair House Hotel. He says he is a retired government worker. He says he is writing a book.

# 1. BLAIR HOUSE

Blair House was on a long thin strip of land that extended into the Tasman Sea. It was a very isolated and lonely place. The house was very large. Chris and Stella Olsen ran Blair House as a private hotel. People chose to stay at Blair House because they liked quiet and beautiful places.

There were no other houses nearby. It was 20km to Walford, a small village with a railway station, a general store and a few houses. If people wanted clothes, alcohol or more variety, they had to drive to a much larger town, Lockton, which was a further 50km north of Walford. From there, one could join the motorway to Auckland.

There was only one road from Walford to Blair House. The road crossed the Blairglen River and went up and over the hills. The road was very narrow, but it didn't matter, because only one van ever drove along it.

One morning, Stella was busy in the kitchen. She was preparing lunch for their guests.

*We will be full,* she thought as she put bowls of salad into the refrigerator. *When Chris comes back with Mr and Mrs Cottingville, we will have ten guests. I'm going to be very busy.*

Stella cooked the meals and did most of the cleaning. Chris helped her. He also looked after their huge vegetable garden and their orchard. He organised activities for their guests. He drove guests to and from the hotel. He did all the shopping. Stella ordered a lot of the food online, but the courier companies would not deliver to such an isolated place. So Chris often drove the 50km to Lockton, to collect the orders from the courier company. In the evenings, he was also the barman.

Chris's brother, Jake, lived with them. He was very strong, and had a beautiful smile. In some ways, Jake was very clever, but he was also different from other people. He could not read or write well. He didn't speak very well. He lived with Stella and Chris because he could not live alone. Jake helped Stella and Chris a lot.

Stella would have liked more staff, but Blair House was a long way from the nearest town, and no one wanted to work there. Stella and Chris worked hard, and got very tired, but mostly, they thought it was a good life. Stella enjoyed meeting the people who came to stay. They were often very interesting.

Stella heard the horn of the van as Chris arrived. She put the last of the salads into the refrigerator, took off her apron and combed her hair. She hurried out to stand on the steps in front of the house.

The van stopped. Chris jumped out and walked around to open the van door for the new guests. A middle-aged couple climbed out. Jake came out to help with the luggage.

"Mr and Mrs Cottingville are in Room Six," Stella said to Jake.

"OK," said Jake, smiling. He picked up four heavy bags and went into the house.

Stella turned to the new guests. "Welcome to Blair House. I hope you will enjoy your stay. I am Stella, and of course, you have met my husband, Chris."

Mr and Mrs Cottingville shook hands. "Please, call me Lou," said the man. He was short and quite fat. He was wearing a heavy gold watch and a thick chain around his neck. He rubbed his hands together as he looked up at the house. He pointed to the woman. "This is Elsa." Elsa was thin. She had very black hair and pale skin. She smiled, but didn't speak.

"Please come this way." Stella led the new guests into the house, while Chris took the van to the garage.

"Did you have a good trip?" asked Stella.

"Yes. It was very easy," answered Lou. "Chris was waiting at the railway station in Walford when we arrived. And we enjoyed the scenery. But I was pleased I didn't have to drive." He laughed. "What a road! So narrow and mountainous!"

"Oh!" said Elsa stopping in the front hallway. "What a beautiful house!" she said, staring at the wood-panelled walls, and the graceful staircase curving upstairs.

"Yes, it is nice, isn't it?" said Stella. "My husband's great-great-uncle built it. He was a very rich man, but he liked to live away from people. So he wanted to build his home in a very lonely place. But we think we are very lucky to live here.

"I'll show you to your room. We'll see you for lunch at twelve thirty. It will be a chance for you to meet our other guests. The dining room is through that door, and the guest lounge and bar are on the other side of the hall."

Stella showed Lou and Elsa to a large pleasant room on the second floor. She showed them their bathroom and the door that led to a balcony outside. Elsa walked out onto the balcony.

"What an amazing view! And we have our own table and chairs. Oh, I see all the rooms open onto the balcony."

"Yes. Please excuse me, I must go and finish preparing lunch."

Stella hurried down the stairs, and back into the kitchen. Jake came to help her carry the food into the dining room. Stella had made soup and homemade bread. There were three different salads, and a platter of cold meats, cheese and fruit.

They put everything on a long table at one side of the room. Chris was waiting to introduce the Cottingvilles to the other guests.

When they walked in, he said. "Breakfast and lunch are self-service. But before you get your food, please let me introduce you to everyone."

## 2. THE GUESTS

Chris took the Cottingvilles around the room. He started with two women in their late thirties who were sitting at a table near a window with a view over the ocean.

"Amy and Ginny. Please meet our new guests, Elsa and Lou Cottingville."

Ginny was very tall and thin. Her black hair was cut very short. Amy was round-faced, with freckles, and a lot of pale red hair. They were both dressed in hiking clothes with heavy walking boots. They smiled and shook hands. "Hi," said Ginny. "This is a great place to stay. I'm sure you'll have a great time."

"Ah, American!" said Lou. "What brings you two ladies so far from home?"

"Birdwatching," said Ginny. "The bird life near here is very special. We are usually out all day, but Amy had a headache this morning. We'll go out after lunch though, won't we, Amy?"

Amy shrugged. It seemed she was not so keen on going out.

A family group was sitting around the next table. A woman, a man who seemed a lot older than her, and a teenage girl playing with a mobile phone. "Wayne and Angela, and their daughter, Chantelle."

"We're here for the fishing," said Angela. She was wearing a lot of makeup. Her T-shirt was low cut and very tight. "Wayne loves fishing, don't you, dear? He goes out to fish whenever the conditions are right. He leaves Chantelle and me here all alone, but that's OK – I have the television and my magazines, and Chantelle just loves horse riding, don't you? Chris takes her out riding most days. She is such a good horsewoman!"

"I like horse riding," said Lou cheerfully. "Maybe I could join you!"

The man at the table nodded and smiled at Elsa and Lou. Chantelle didn't even look up. She stared at her phone. Her long brown hair covered most of her face and she looked rather sulky.

Chris shrugged and moved towards a table in the middle of the room. "Our author! Max, meet Elsa and Lou." Max rose to his feet. He was an older man, tall and tanned, and very well dressed. He shook hands. "Delighted to meet you. I'm not an author, you know, but I am trying to write a book. If I can get it published, I will call myself an author. But for now, I am just a retired government worker, who spends his days writing and walking."

A middle-aged couple were sitting at the last table. They were both very overweight and were dressed in matching purple tracksuits. They seemed to be strange guests for a hotel that attracted people who liked nature and outdoor exercise.

"Delia and Gilbert," said Chris. Delia looked towards the buffet table. "The food's getting cold," she said. "You'll like it here. Stella is a very good chef, and the beds are comfortable."

"Yes," nodded Gilbert, "And Chris has a very good selection of wines."

"Where would you like to sit?" Chris asked Lou and Elsa. They looked around the room. Elsa started to walk towards an empty table, but Lou walked over to Amy and Ginny's table. Elsa looked disappointed, but she followed her husband.

"Can we join you?" asked Lou. "I'd like to hear about these birds of yours."

Amy and Ginny did not look pleased, but they smiled and nodded.

"Now everyone," said Chris. "I see Stella has brought lunch out. Please help yourselves. Stella will bring dessert and tea and coffee shortly. If you need anything, ring the bell," he said to Lou and Elsa. He showed them the bell by the dining room door. "We'll be in the kitchen. I hope you enjoy your lunch."

Back in the kitchen, Jake was sitting at the table having soup. He smiled at Chris. "Good soup!" he said.

Stella served Chris, and put a platter of bread and cheese on the table.

She stood by the kitchen counter and drank some soup from a

mug. "Are you OK?" asked Chris.

"Yes. Yes, I'm fine. Just a bit tired, and I still have to prepare dinner for tonight."

"Jake and I will clear the dining room and do the dishes for you," said Chris.

"But you were away all morning. Don't you have to take Chantelle horse riding? And won't the Cottingvilles want to be taken out for a walk or something?"

Chris laughed. "Chantelle doesn't want to go horse riding. She only says she wants to go riding so she can escape from her mother. She puts on her riding clothes, walks down to the horse paddock and hides in one of the stables. She spends all her time on her phone or iPad. It's our little secret."

"And the Cottingvilles?"

"When I was driving them here, I asked them what they wanted to do. Fishing? Kayaking? Mountain biking? Walking? Rock climbing? Horse riding? They said maybe in a few days, but for now, they just want to relax."

"Do you know how long they plan to stay?" asked Stella.

"No. You took the reservation. A week?"

"Yes, but they also said maybe longer or shorter."

"It's good for us if they stay for more than a week," said Chris, helping himself to bread and cheese.

"Chris?" said Stella thoughtfully. "Do you ever wonder why people come here to stay?"

"What do you mean?"

"Well, we have ten people staying here. They are all very different. I understand why Max is here. He walks. He works on his book. Amy and Ginny go bird watching. But some of them, like Angela, and Delia and Gilbert don't like nature or outdoor activities. Delia and Gilbert just eat, drink and sleep. The Cottingvilles seem like typical city people too, and they don't want to do anything. Why are they here?"

Chris stood up and hugged Stella. "Well, Lou said he liked horse riding, and Delia and Gilbert are here for the food. You are such a great cook. Angela and Chantelle don't have any choice. Wayne is here to fish. She talks all the time, and he says nothing, but I guess they have to do what he wants. You think too much. Are dessert and the tea and coffee ready? Jake and I will take them in."

"Yes." Stella pointed to the plates of homemade cakes, and the pots of tea and coffee.

The men disappeared towards the dining room. *Even so,* thought Stella. *I don't think Wayne knows anything about fishing. The times he goes out to fish are all wrong. Anyone who has done even a little fishing, knows more than he does.*

## 3. CHRIS GOES TO THE CITY

At 7:00pm, all the guests were in the bar. This was an old conservatory next to the guest lounge. There were comfortable armchairs and sofas, a piano and a pool table. Big glass doors separated the conservatory from the lounge, so when they were open, it was one large room.

Chris was behind the bar counter serving juice, cocktails, beer, and wine. The bar had opened at 5:30pm. Most guests arrived just before the dinnertime of 7:30pm. But Angela was always early. She was drinking cocktails. She always drank a lot. The more she drank, the more she talked. Wayne was drinking water. Amy and Ginny were sitting away from the others as usual. Ginny was drinking beer, and Amy had a glass of wine and soda.

Lou was also drinking beer and talking to everyone.

*He's a very sociable guy,* thought Chris. *We like our guests to talk to each other. It's one of the things that make a small private hotel special. But he asks too many questions. Some of our guests are very private people. I hope he's not going to annoy them, and I wonder about Elsa. She's not talking, but she's drinking almost as much as Angela.*

Jake was in the kitchen with Stella. He was sitting at the table playing on his PlayStation. Stella looked at the plates of food on the table. "Jake," she said. "Will you take these snacks through to the bar, please?"

"Wait," said Jake. He was in the middle of a game. His face was screwed up, and his fingers and thumbs were moving quickly. "Yes!" he said.

"Can you help now?" asked Stella. "Can you take these snacks through to the bar?" "OK," said Jake. Stella gave him two trays of bruschetta, choux pastries and melon balls, and he disappeared out the door.

Stella turned back to her meal. The first course was smoked trout salad and she arranged the servings on separate plates for each guest. Delia and Gilbert's plates had more food than the others. Stella knew that if she gave them the same amount as other people, they would ask for more. So it was easier to make their salads bigger from the start.

The venison was in the oven with the red cabbage side dish. The port and redcurrant sauce was warming on the stove and the creamed potatoes would only need a few moments in the microwave. Everything was ready.

Jake was back in the kitchen. He and Stella carried the trout salads to the side-table in the dining room. Then Stella went into the bar and said, "Dinner is ready." When everyone was seated, Chris helped Stella serve the salads to each guest, and took their drink orders. Stella hurried back to the kitchen to be ready to serve the main course and the dessert course.

After serving berry tarts with Chantilly cream, and putting cheese, fruit and crackers on every table, Stella was finally free to sit in the kitchen. *I'm tired,* she thought. *But the meal was good. Now, I have to think about tomorrow's meals. At least breakfast is easy.*

She sat at the table and ate a few leftovers. She had left a plate of food for Jake on the table earlier. He ate, and disappeared to his bedroom with his PlayStation. His room was on the ground floor next to Stella and Chris's bedroom.

Chris came back and said, "I can serve coffee now. Is it ready?" Stella waved at the brewed coffee, cream, sugar and chocolates. Chris took everything out to the dining room and came back. "Your food was amazing as usual. You did a great job. But you must be tired," he said.

"Yes," said Stella. "I'm tired, but I want to check my emails. I had no time earlier today. "OK," said Chris. He went to their room and came back with their laptops. "Here we are."

Stella used her laptop for the hotel business. She used it for reservations, accounts and shopping. She sorted through the emails. There were advertisements, bills, and enquiries from people wanting to stay.

Then Stella looked at the travel sites they used. Stella read all the comments posted by guests. They all said the same sort of things. We had a wonderful time... The service was great... We loved the activities... We loved your food... We will come again...

Stella was reading the comments out to Chris. "They all say good things!" she said.

Chris didn't answer. He was reading something on his computer. His face had gone white. "I have to go to Auckland," he said.

"Why?" asked Stella. "What are you reading? Is it an email?"

"Yes. It doesn't matter. Don't worry. I'm going to Auckland," said Chris.

"When?" asked Stella.

"Now. I will be back tomorrow."

Chris shut down his computer. He got up from the table and went to their bedroom. Stella followed him. "What are you doing?"

She watched Chris throw his best suit, a shirt and tie, socks and business shoes, into a bag. He grabbed his toothbrush and razor from their bathroom, and put them into the bag.

Chris hugged Stella. "I'm sorry. I love you. You'll be OK. Look after Jake. I will come back tomorrow."

He walked out the door to the back of the house. Stella stood at the kitchen door. She heard Chris drive the van down the drive and out onto the hill road.

She ran around the house, and saw the van disappear into the darkness.

*What was in that email? What's happening?* Stella was very frightened.

Just then the bell rang from the dining room. It was Delia. "Can we have more coffee?" she asked. "And maybe some cream?"

"Of course," said Stella. "Just a minute."

Stella made more coffee and took it to the dining room.

"Your meal was delicious," said Delia.

"Yes, it was very good," said Max. It seemed everyone was very pleased with the meal. Stella was happy, but she wanted everyone to go to bed.

Finally, all the guests went upstairs. Stella cleared the dishes and washed them. She cleaned the dining room and prepared the side-table for breakfast. Usually she had Chris to help her, but tonight she had to do everything alone.

## Trapped

It was midnight when Stella finished all her work and went to bed. She was so tired she fell asleep at once.

## 4. A CHANGE IN THE WEATHER

The alarm went off at 5:00am. Stella woke instantly. She felt strange. She and Chris had been married for 15 years, and they had never spent a night apart. *What was in that email? He wouldn't show me. He packed a bag and drove off in the middle of the night. I don't like this. Something is very wrong.*

She sighed. *I can't worry about it now. I have too much to do.*

She showered, dressed and hurried to the kitchen. Most mornings she used the time from 5:30am to 7:30am to prepare most of the food for the day's meals. Then she prepared breakfast, which was available to the guests from 8:00am to 9:00am. While the guests were eating, she cleaned the bar and guest lounge.

After she had cleared and cleaned the dining room, it was time to clean the guest rooms and bathrooms. Usually, Chris helped her until about 10:00am when the guests were ready for their outdoor activities. Some days he drove to Walford, or even as far as Lockton to go to the bank, collect online orders and to buy any fruit and vegetables that they did not grow themselves.

Stella turned on the coffeemaker in the kitchen, and started pulling food out of the refrigerator and the big cool room next to the back verandah. When the coffee was done, she poured herself a cup and sat down to send a text to Chris. *I can't expect to hear from him for a while. I hope he's sleeping. He wouldn't have got to Auckland until after midnight.*

While Stella and Jake were delivering breakfast to the dining room, both Max and Delia asked her where Chris was. She said the same to each of them. "He's got an unexpected business meeting in Auckland. He left last night, so that he would be there on time. He'll be back later today."

Chantelle overheard Stella and asked loudly, "But what about my horse riding?"

Stella smiled to herself. *You mean your time away from your mother hiding out near the stables.* But she said, "Oh Chantelle, I'm sorry. I'm sure Chris will take you out tomorrow. Perhaps you could go down and say 'hi' to the horses anyway."

"Oh good. That won't take you long," said Angela. "And then you and I can have a great day together. How about we give each other a pedicure?"

Chantelle rolled her eyes, but didn't answer.

"If anyone plans to go out today, I suggest you do it this morning, or early afternoon," said Max. "I checked the weather forecast on my computer before I came down to breakfast, and we have some very bad weather coming this way."

"Oh, really?" said Lou. "It looks perfect out there." Everyone turned to look outside, and it seemed to be a very beautiful day. There was no wind. The sun was shining, and the water and sky were a deep blue.

"Even so, by late afternoon, the storm will arrive. We can expect at least twelve hours of strong winds and rain," said Max.

Ginny said to Amy, "We should go out as soon as possible after breakfast. We must make the most of the good weather." She turned to Stella. "Do you think you could make us a picnic lunch?"

"Of course," said Stella. "No problem."

"Oh, I'd like one too," said Wayne. "And me," said Lou. "I think I'll take a long walk."

"I'll go and prepare them now," said Stella, smiling. "What would you like to drink with your picnics?"

"Just water for us," said Ginny.

"Could I have a thermos of coffee?" asked Wayne. "If it's not too much trouble."

"Same for me." Lou was eating his breakfast quickly. He seemed to be in a hurry.

Stella made up the picnic lunches of sandwiches, cake and fruit, and left them on the table in the front hall.

The morning went smoothly. As usual, Jake did everything she asked. He carried towels and bed linen to the laundry, and helped vacuum and sweep all the floors. Stella had her mobile phone in her apron pocket. She had just finished the bedrooms when it beeped to indicate a text message. It was from Chris.

---*Everything is fine. Don't worry, but it's taking longer than I thought. I might be very late back tonight. Can you manage OK?*---

---*Yes of course*--- Stella texted back.

---*Will explain everything when I get back. Will be in meetings, so maybe can't text until later today. Love you, C*---

Lunch was a quiet meal. Max did not appear. Stella was not surprised. He often stayed in his room working through the day, or came back mid-afternoon from one of his long walks. Only Delia, Gilbert, Angela and Chantelle were in the big dining room enjoying the quiche and salads Stella had prepared. Chantelle sat hunched up over her phone. She ate nothing, and Stella thought she had been crying.

*She is a very annoying teenager. She is not very polite, and I think she is selfish. But I do feel sorry for her. She doesn't have a good relationship with her mother. Angela is such a silly woman. And it's not a very exciting place for a young person. I wonder where Elsa is? Maybe she went out with Lou. I didn't make her any lunch, but Lou's picnic box would be enough for two.*

It was mid-afternoon when the wind and rain started. Delia and Gilbert were sleeping in the guest lounge, where Angela was flicking through TV channels. Chantelle was nowhere to be seen. Wayne, Amy and Ginny had come back to the house before it rained and were in their rooms. As the afternoon passed, the sky got blacker and blacker. The rain was very heavy. The wind got stronger and howled around the big old house. By 5:00pm, it was as dark as night outside.

## 5. NO PHONE, NO INTERNET

Stella was taking food out of the refrigerator for the evening meal, when Chantelle appeared in the kitchen. "I don't have a phone signal," she said.

Her mother appeared behind her. "There is no Sky on the TV. I was watching one of my favourite shows! You'll have to fix it."

"Oh dear," said Stella. "We have our own cell tower. Maybe it has got damaged in the wind. I'll go and see."

"You can't go out in this storm," said Chantelle. "It's too dangerous."

"I'm only going up to the top of the house," said Stella. "I will be able to see the tower from the window in your room. Is it OK if I go in there to look?"

"Sure. I'll come with you," said Chantelle.

As they walked up the stairs, the house shook in the wind and the windows rattled.

*It's the first time Chantelle has shown any concern for anyone,* thought Stella. *Maybe I misjudged her.*

They stood at the window of Chantelle's room, and looked out at the hill behind the house. "It's gone," said Stella. "It must have fallen down. That means no cell phones, no Internet, and no TV. I'm sorry."

They left the room and went back downstairs in silence. Stella sighed. "I'll have to tell everyone. I guess they will be very annoyed. At least we still have electricity. The main generator's still going, and we have a back-up as well."

Stella went into the guest lounge. Angela was drumming her fingers on a magazine and staring at the TV as though the picture would suddenly appear. Gilbert and Delia were still asleep in armchairs. Wayne was standing staring out the window at the storm.

Stella explained about the cell tower. "I am so sorry. But Chris should be able to solve the problem when he gets back."

Angela looked very annoyed. "I think it's very bad. We expect to have television and telephones and Internet. Why don't you call someone to come and fix it?"

"It's after five pm. If Chris can't fix it, we will call a company to come. But no one will be willing to come until tomorrow."

"It's not good enough," said Angela. "Don't expect to be paid for our stay. And I will post very negative reports about this hotel on the Internet!"

"Oh really, Angela," shouted Wayne. "As if Stella is responsible for the weather! This is a very bad storm. We'll be lucky if nothing else is damaged. So why don't you shut up and read one of those stupid magazines of yours?"

Stella was very surprised. Wayne almost never spoke, and seemed to ignore his wife all the time. *This is something new,* she thought. *Maybe the weather has upset him. I know that some people don't like storms.*

"I must go and tell everyone else," she said.

Stella went back upstairs and knocked on Lou and Elsa's door. There was no answer. Next, she tried Amy and Ginny's door. There was no answer, but she could hear sounds of someone moving and quiet voices. She knocked again. She heard the key turn in the lock. *Who locks their door during daytime when they're in their room?*

The door opened just a little, and she saw Ginny's face. "What do you want?"

"I'm sorry to disturb you," said Stella. She explained about the cell tower. "I hope it won't be inconvenient for you."

"It's OK. We won't come down for dinner tonight. Amy doesn't feel like it."

"Is she OK? Is she ill?"

"No. She's just tired."

"I'll send your meals up to you at dinner time. You can eat in your room."

"Thanks," said Ginny and shut the door immediately.

Stella turned to go downstairs and jumped. Max was standing in the hallway behind her. "Oh, you frightened me," she said. "I was coming to see you too, to explain about the cell tower."

"I heard you telling Ginny," said Max. "It doesn't make things easy for you, does it?"

"No. But I can't do anything about it."

Max walked down the stairs with Stella. "I suppose Angela is very angry."

Stella smiled a little, "Yes. She is."

"And Chris has not returned?"

"No. And I don't know when he will arrive. He said maybe he would be delayed in town. Crossing the hills in this weather would be quite dangerous. So I hope he doesn't try."

Max looked at his watch. "The bar should be open."

*Oh no!* thought Stella. *I had forgotten about the bar. Chris always does that, and I have dinner to cook. What am I going to do?*

Max was speaking. "I will be your barman for tonight."

"I can't ask you to do that!" Stella was shocked. "You are a guest."

"You are not asking. I am volunteering. Many years ago, I had a part-time job as a barman. I will enjoy it, and I have a good reason to do it."

"Oh. What's that?"

"It will cheer Angela up, and we won't have to listen to her complaining."

Stella laughed. "OK. And thank you very much. It will help me a lot!"

Stella hurried towards the kitchen. Then she thought, *Where are Elsa and Lou? I haven't seen them. Never mind. I'll find them later. But I must find Jake now. He hates loud noises, and maybe he is frightened.*

Stella found Jake in the kitchen. He had a blanket over his head and was playing a game on his PlayStation. *At least Jake can play his games,* she thought. *And we can recharge his PlayStation.*

She spoke softly to Jake, and left him under his blanket.

Then, with a sigh, she started preparing the food for dinner. Usually Stella loved to cook, but that evening it seemed too difficult. Chantelle came into the kitchen.

"Can I help you?" she asked.

"Oh no. I'm fine."

"I want to!" Chantelle seemed very angry. "I can't stay out there!"

*I wonder why,* thought Stella. *Maybe it is better not to ask.*

Chantelle sat at the table next to Jake. She patted the blanket. "Hello, Jake," she said quietly.

Jake's face appeared from under the blanket. His face lit up with his beautiful smile. "Chantelle," he said. Then he pulled the blanket back over his head.

"I can't do very much, but I could peel some potatoes, or chop some vegetables," said Chantelle.

"Your mother will be very angry," said Stella.

"I don't care! Angela is a witch! I don't care if she is angry with me."

"But she will be angry with me," said Stella.

"I won't tell her. And Jake won't tell her. And you won't tell her. Please!"

"OK. It has been a difficult day, and I would love some help. But you must tie your hair up and wear an apron."

Stella gave Chantelle a clean apron. Chantelle pulled her hair up and tied it in a tight knot on top of her head.

"There are tomatoes in the vegetable drawer. Can you cut about six of them into very small pieces?"

Chantelle was smiling.

*I have never seen her smile. She is very pretty when she smiles. The poor girl, I wonder why her life is so difficult?*

Stella had never had help in the kitchen before. Chantelle had no cooking experience, but she could stir sauces, and wash, peel and chop vegetables. The preparations for dinner went very fast. Stella and Chantelle made tiny sandwiches, dips and raw vegetables, for pre-dinner snacks.

At 6:30pm the snacks were ready, dinner was cooking and the desserts were in refrigerator. Stella poured cokes for Chantelle and Jake.

"You have helped me so much. I'll take the snacks out to the bar. We don't want your mother to see you. Please relax for a few minutes. And please see if you can get Jake to drink something," she said to Chantelle.

## 6. A PARTY

The bar was very noisy. Everyone was talking very loudly. Stella walked over to Max. "Is everything OK?" she asked.

"Oh, yes," he said. "I'm a very good barman. Look!"

Stella looked around the room. The storm was very loud, and the wind made the windows rattle, but no one in the bar seemed to notice.

Angela's face was red. She was sitting at a table with Gilbert and Delia. Angela was talking, and it seemed that Delia and Gilbert were interested in what she was saying. Elsa was sitting alone at another table. She was looking out the window at the storm. Wayne and Lou were playing pool.

"So everyone is here, except Ginny and Amy," said Stella.

Max shrugged. "The weather is so bad. Maybe people feel better with company.

Where's Chantelle?"

"Don't worry about Chantelle," said Stella. "She's OK. And thank you! You are doing a great job!"

Stella took the trays of snacks to the guests.

On her way back to the kitchen, she thought, *I wonder when Lou came in? And where was Elsa all day? I didn't see her.*

Back in the kitchen, Chantelle helped Stella with the last stages of the meal.

"Go now," said Stella to Chantelle. "You must join the other guests for dinner."

Chantelle sighed. "OK. But I like it better out here with you and

Jake."

She left the kitchen and Stella got ready to serve. She took a tray of food up to Amy and Ginny's room. She knocked. "Dinner!" she called out.

"Leave it outside the door," Ginny shouted. Stella put the tray on a table in the hallway.

Jake wouldn't move from under his blanket, so Stella took the first courses out to the big side-table, and went into the bar. "I'm sorry everyone," she said. "But Chris isn't here, so I can't do everything. Could you collect your meals from the side-table please?"

"Well, really!" said Angela. "I think we deserve better service than that!"

Wayne sighed and put down his pool cue. "Come and eat, Angela. I'll bring your meal to you."

The meal was a success, but Stella was exhausted when she finally took the tea and coffee into the dining room.

She went back to the kitchen and started rinsing the dishes, glasses and cutlery. Chantelle appeared and silently helped Stella load the dishwasher and clean the kitchen.

"You shouldn't be here," said Stella. "Your mother will be angry."

"She will be too drunk to notice," said Chantelle.

Stella was too tired to argue, so she let Chantelle help.

When everything was done, Stella put a plate of food on the table near Jake. Usually Jake was hungry, but tonight he stayed under his blanket.

"Can I get you anything?" she asked Chantelle.

"No. I'm fine. If I want a drink may I get a coke from the refrigerator?"

"Sure," smiled Stella. "There are cakes and cookies in the pantry. Take anything you want. I must go and see if anyone wants more tea or coffee."

The dining room was empty. Everyone was back in the bar. There was a party in progress. It was very noisy. Everyone was laughing and talking. Lou and Delia were standing next to the piano. Gilbert was playing a jazz tune. It sounded very good. As Stella went to talk to Max behind the bar, Gilbert changed to *Cry Me a River*, and Lou and Delia started to sing.

Over at the bar, Max smiled at Stella. "Everything is fine," he said softly. "Why don't you go to bed?"

"I can't do that!" Stella was shocked.

"Yes, you can. I have the bar under control. Lou is the life and soul of the party. Everyone is having a good time. Go to bed."

"But I have to clean up in here when they finish."

"No, you don't. I'll take all the glasses out to the kitchen. I'm not going to wash them, but you can do that in the morning."

Stella's head was hurting, and she was very, very tired.

"OK. If you're sure?"

"I'm sure. Now go."

"Bless you, Max," she said.

Back in the kitchen, Chantelle was sitting next to Jake. He had come out from under his blanket, and was eating cake. Chantelle had cokes on the table. They seemed very relaxed. Just then, there was a very strong wind gust. The old house shook, and all the windows and doors rattled.

Jake pulled his blanket back over his head.

"Time to go to bed, Jake," said Stella.

She took Jake by the arm and persuaded him to stand up. She walked with him along the hallway to his room. Chantelle followed them carrying the PlayStation. When they got there, Jake lay down on his bed and put his pillows over his head. Chantelle looked around and found the charger for the PlayStation. She plugged it in.

"He'll want it in the morning," she said. "I guess I should go and find Angela."

Stella hugged her. "You have been so much help," she said. "Thank you!"

Chantelle shrugged. "That's OK." She went back to the guests' area and Stella went to her bedroom.

Chris was not back. Stella hoped he wouldn't try to drive in the storm. *Oh Chris, I miss you,* she thought. *And I can't even text you, or send an email.*

In five minutes she had changed into nightwear, cleaned her teeth and fallen into bed. A minute later, she was asleep.

## 7. HORROR IN THE MORNING

Something woke Stella up. She rolled over and looked at the alarm clock. *4:45am.* She switched the alarm off, and listened. It was morning. The storm had died out in the night, and it was very quiet. Too quiet. Then she heard it. A woman was screaming. The noise was coming from outside.

Stella jumped out of bed and pulled on a sweatshirt and jeans. She ran outside. Ginny was kneeling on the ground. She was screaming. "Amy! Amy!"

As Stella ran towards Ginny, she saw that Ginny was holding Amy in her arms. Amy's eyes were open, her head was rolled back, and her pale red hair was lying over the ground.

At the same time, Max came around the corner of the house. They reached Ginny together. He put his arms around Ginny and forced her to let go of Amy. Stella knelt down next to Amy. She wanted to help her. "Don't touch her!" said Max. "Look after Ginny."

Stella tried to pull Ginny away, but Ginny was very strong, and she was still screaming. Finally, Stella was able to pull Ginny a few metres away. She put her arms around her. Ginny suddenly stopped screaming and started crying quietly. But she struggled, and tried to run back to Amy.

Stella watched Max. He knelt over the body and put his fingers on Amy's neck. *He's done this before,* thought Stella. *Is he a doctor? No. He said he was a retired government worker.*

Stella jumped. Someone was standing behind her. It was Delia. "There's been an accident?" she asked. "Let me take Ginny." Delia came forward and put her arms around Ginny. "Come with me, dear," she said. "We can't do anything here. Come inside and sit down."

Ginny went with Delia like an upset child with its mother.

Stella watched Delia take Ginny into the house. Now Gilbert, Wayne and Chantelle were standing behind her. They were all looking at Max.

*The noise must have woken them up too,* thought Stella.

Gilbert walked over to join Max. He knelt down next to him. The two men spoke very quietly. Then Max stood up. "She's dead," he said. "I need something to cover the body."

"Uh. We have some big plastic sheets in the laundry," said Stella.

"I'll get one," said Chantelle. She ran to the house, and soon came back carrying a big sheet of strong plastic.

Gilbert took the plastic sheet from Chantelle, and went to join Max next to Amy's dead body. They covered the body.

*Chantelle!* thought Stella. *This is a bad situation for a young girl!*

"Chantelle!" she said. "Why are you here? Please go back into the house. This is not a good place for you!"

"No," said Chantelle. "I'm staying here."

"Wayne," said Stella. "This is not a good situation for Chantelle. Please tell your daughter to go inside."

Max's voice sounded very loud. "Everyone. Into the house, now! I want everyone in the dining room."

"We can't leave Amy here alone!" said Stella.

"Yes we can. We must. We can't do anything for her. I want everyone inside, and in the dining room. Chantelle, wake your mother up. Wayne. Can you please go and ask Lou and Elsa to come to the dining room? Stella. Go now!"

Stella was surprised. Max was always very quiet and calm, but now he was very strong.

They all walked back into the house. Stella felt someone pulling at the sleeve of her sweatshirt. It was Chantelle. "Please. Can you go and wake Angela? I'll go and get Jake. I guess he heard the noise and is hiding in his room."

"OK," said Stella. *I don't know why Chantelle does not want to wake her mother, but everything today is strange. So I won't think about it.*

Stella hurried upstairs and knocked on Angela's door.

*Wayne was downstairs. The noise woke him up. Why is Angela still sleeping? Why didn't Wayne wake her up?*

There was no answer, so Stella opened the door. There was a strong smell of alcohol. She looked at the bed. Angela was lying on her back. She was snoring.

*She is still drunk!* thought Stella. She walked to the bed. She shook Angela. "Wake up!" she said. "You must come to the dining room now!"

Angela didn't move, so Stella shook her harder. "Wake up!" she shouted. Finally, Angela opened her eyes. "What do you want?" she asked Stella.

"Get up! Take a shower! Get dressed! Come to the dining room! Hurry! Amy has died!"

"Who?"

"Amy!"

As Stella walked out of the room, she heard Angela get out of the bed.

Stella went downstairs and into the kitchen.

*Coffee, tea, some food,* she thought. She made tea and coffee. She went to the pantry and took out boxes of cake and cookies. Chantelle came into the kitchen. She was holding Jake's hand. He was wearing clean clothes.

"Jake is good this morning!" smiled Chantelle.

Jake looked happy. "No wind! No noise!"

"Thank you, Chantelle!"

*I love this girl,* thought Stella. "Do you want to change before we meet in the dining room?"

Chantelle looked down at her clothes. She was wearing a very small T-shirt and tiny cotton shorts. She laughed. "OK. Maybe I am not wearing enough clothes. I'll come back soon."

Stella turned to Jake. "Help me please."

"OK," said Jake. He helped Stella take everything into the dining room. Gilbert and Max were already there.

"I must talk to everyone," said Max. "Wayne has gone upstairs to tell Elsa and Lou to come down here."

Stella said, "Please get tea and coffee," she said. "There is some bread, and cake and cookies. I'm sorry I haven't made breakfast, but it is still very early."

*What am I saying?* she asked herself. *Amy has died, and I am talking like a waitress!*

"Please sit down, Stella," said Max. "Jake. Please sit down with Stella."

Jake was confused. He never sat down in the dining room.

"It's OK," said Stella. "Come and sit down with me. Max wants to tell us a story."

"OK," Jake smiled. "I like stories!"

## 8. MAX IN CHARGE

Stella looked around the room. Max was sitting at a table near the window.

Gilbert was taking hot drinks to Ginny and Delia, who were sitting at another table in the middle of the room. Ginny's head was down on the table and Delia had her arm around her shoulders.

Stella poured herself a cup of coffee, and led Jake to a table in the corner. She watched Gilbert sit down next to Max. Chantelle walked into the room wearing jeans and a long-sleeved shirt. She sat alone on the same side of the room as Jake and Stella.

"I don't see why I had to get up and dressed! Really, what kind of hotel is this?" Angela marched into the room with Wayne behind her. "First of all, I get woken up by all the noise outside! I had only just gone back to sleep, when Stella comes to our room and says I have to come to the dining room immediately!" She turned and glared at Wayne. "Then you come back to the room, and say the same thing!"

"Come and sit down, Angela," said Wayne quietly. "I'll get you some coffee. But you must sit down and listen. I'm sure there's a very good reason why Max wants us here."

He took Angela's arm and forced her to sit at one of the tables. "Stay there. And please stop talking."

Wayne moved to the buffet table, but he stopped next to Chantelle. He spoke quietly, but Stella heard him say, "Are you OK?"

Chantelle nodded.

"Good morning, everyone!" Lou came in smiling and rubbing his hands. Elsa was with him. "Do we have a surprise? It was a great party last night, wasn't it? So, what are we going to do today? It must be important, since we have to get up so early!"

He looked around the room. "Why does everyone look so serious?"

"Please get yourselves something to eat and drink," said Max. "Then I will tell you."

Lou walked over to the side-table, humming the song he and Delia had sung the night before. Elsa followed him silently.

*I haven't heard her say a word since lunchtime on the day they arrived,* thought Stella. *She seemed OK when they first came here, but now she doesn't speak or look at anyone. I wonder what has happened?*

When everyone was sitting down, Max stood up.

"Please listen, everyone." He looked around the room.

"Amy died during the night. Ginny found her body on the ground below their room."

Everyone turned to stare at Ginny. She didn't raise her head, but she made a sound like a wild animal.

"We can't call the police, so we must do the best we can, until someone can go into Walford for help." He looked at Stella.

"Chris is away with the van. What other transport options do we have?" he asked.

"Well. There's the four-wheel motorbike that Chris uses in the garden and orchard. But Chris will be back soon. Can't we wait until he arrives?"

"I don't think so," said Max. "I think we should contact the police as soon as possible."

"Why?" asked Wayne. "Surely it was just a terrible accident. Amy must have fallen off the balcony. Can't we wait until Chris comes back?"

"He should have arrived by now, and he hasn't," said Max. "We don't know why, and he can't get a message to us because the cell phone tower is broken. We must act now."

Max turned to Gilbert and spoke softly.

Gilbert nodded, got up, and left the room.

"Can I have my breakfast now?" asked Angela. "I don't know why you think you are in charge here. It's very sad that Amy had an accident and died. But it doesn't mean we have to suffer. It's bad enough we have no Internet and no TV, but Stella could at least feed us properly."

"I'm sorry, Angela," said Stella standing up. "I'll make some breakfast for everyone now."

"Sit down, Stella," said Max loudly. Stella was very surprised, but she sat down.

"I want everyone to tell me exactly what you did last night. From the time you left the bar, until this morning."

"Stella. You go first. Tell me everything."

*What is this?* Stella wondered. *Why does it matter what I did?*

"When I left the bar, I went to the kitchen and took Jake to his bedroom. I made sure he went to bed. Then I went to my bedroom. I was very tired. I fell asleep. The noise outside woke me up at about four forty-five am."

"Thank you, Stella," said Max.

He turned to look at Wayne. "Wayne. Please tell us what you did last night."

"Oh. Angela and I left the bar about midnight. We went upstairs to our room. Angela fell asleep. I sat on the sofa and read for a while. I fell asleep on the sofa."

"Did you hear anything?"

"Hear what?" Wayne looked puzzled.

Max shrugged. "Did you hear any strange noises? Anything different from other nights?"

"No. Yes." Wayne seemed uncomfortable. He looked across at Ginny. "Um. I heard shouting. It came from Amy and Ginny's room. That was when I was reading."

"Did you hear who was shouting?"

Stella thought this was an important question. Max's face was very serious.

Wayne was unhappy. "Uh. The voices were women's voices. I thought it was Amy and Ginny. I don't know."

"It was us," said Ginny. Everyone jumped. Ginny lifted her head from the table. "We had a terrible fight. I came down to the guest lounge, and slept on a sofa. I woke up about four thirty and went back upstairs. Amy wasn't in our room. I didn't know where she was. The doors to the balcony were open. I went out there and looked. I saw her on the ground! I ran downstairs and she was dead! Dead! And it's my fault!"

Ginny was screaming and crying. She was banging her hands on the table. Delia was trying to calm her down. Then just as suddenly as she had started talking, she stopped. She put her head on the table and cried.

Max asked Chantelle, Delia and Angela to tell him what they did the night before. He also asked them if they had heard anything. They all said almost the thing. They had gone to bed, gone to sleep. They had not heard anything until they were woken up by Ginny screaming.

## 9. MORE BAD NEWS

Max was just asking Elsa and Lou the same questions, when Gilbert came back into the room. He walked over to Max. He spoke very quietly into Max's ear.

Stella looked around the room. Elsa was sitting with Lou, but she was looking out the window. Lou was watching Max. He seemed to think the situation was amusing. He was whistling through his teeth.

*What an awful man he is,* thought Stella. *He is so cheerful. He made sure everyone had a good time at the party last night, but he doesn't seem to care about Amy.*

Angela lit a cigarette. There was a strict no smoking rule at Blair House, but Stella thought it was not a good time to say anything. Delia was stroking Ginny's back, and talking to her quietly. *I thought she was only interested in eating,* thought Stella. *But now I can see she is a very nice, kind woman. Who are these people? Why are they here? Max has taken charge. Why? He has made a team with Gilbert. They know something. What is it?* Stella felt very cold.

Max spoke. "Gilbert went to the garage. The four-wheel motorbike has been badly damaged. Gilbert looked at the mountain bikes too. The tyres have been cut, and all the spare tyres as well. Then Gilbert had a good idea. He thought maybe we could use the kayaks to go along the coast to Walford. He went down to the boathouse. All the kayaks have holes in them. Someone does not want us to get out of this place."

Stella thought that everyone would start talking and shouting. It was very strange. No one said anything.

"I can ride to Walford," said Chantelle.

"What?" said Wayne. "I can't let you do that."

"Why not?" asked Chantelle. She looked very young, but very strong. "I can take a horse and ride to Walford.

Max looked at Chantelle. "Can you do this?" he asked.

"Yes I can." Chantelle sounded very confident.

She is so young, but she is very brave, thought Stella.

Max smiled at Chantelle.

"OK. But, if you ride to Walford, I think someone should go with you. I could go, but I want to stay here. Are there any volunteers? Who is a good rider?"

"Lou said he likes riding," said Wayne. "Lou, you could go. Why don't you ride to Walford?"

Everyone looked at Lou. He drank some of his coffee, took a bite of cake and said, "No. I don't think so. Who do you think you are Max? I'll tell you. You're someone who has never done anything. Now you think you can control us all. It's crazy. Amy fell off the balcony. It was an accident, but now you are making a drama out of it. Do you want to put it in your book? You are making a lot of fuss about nothing. No. I'm going to have my breakfast, and stay here." He smiled at everyone and ate some more cake.

"I could go with Chantelle. But I have to stay here. It will take four or five hours to ride to Walford. Chris is not here, and I have to …" Stella couldn't decide what to do.

Max spoke again. "When I saw Amy's body this morning, I didn't think she died from a fall. Gilbert knows about these things. He agrees with me. Someone broke Amy's neck and pushed her body off the balcony. She was murdered. And someone here is the murderer."

Again, there was silence. Stella felt weak. *What is happening? Where is Chris?* She looked around the room. *One of these people killed Amy! Who?*

Angela started shouting. "Murder! Amy was murdered! We all know who did it!"

She ran towards Stella and Jake. She pointed at Jake. "It was him! He's not normal. He did it! And now he's going to murder me! Get him! Lock him up. Tell the police!"

Wayne jumped up, but Chantelle was quicker.

She stood between Jake and Angela. "You are a crazy woman! Jake is my friend. He could not hurt anyone! He did not kill Amy. He will not kill you! I will kill you!"

Stella put her arms around Jake. "Chantelle. I know this is very difficult. But you must not talk to your mother like this."

"My mother! Are you joking? She is a witch, and she is not my mother!" Chantelle started crying, and ran out of the room. Stella wanted to follow her, but she had to look after Jake. He hated loud noises, and he was very upset.

"Why is everyone shouting?" he asked. "Why is Chantelle sad?"

Stella held onto Jake. *Oh Chris! Where are you? This is too much for me!*

Delia spoke. "Stella. Lou won't go, and no one else can ride well enough to go to Walford. I will look after everything here. I can cook something, and Gilbert will help me."

"Can you cook?" asked Stella.

"Of course I can cook! Do you think I would be as fat as this if I didn't cook? You are the best person to ride to Walford. So go."

"But Ginny. Someone must look after Ginny!"

"I will take her up to our room," said Delia. "And I will give her a sleeping tablet. I am sure she will sleep."

Max looked worried. "I think someone should sit with her."

Elsa looked away from the window. "I will sit with Ginny." She walked over to the table and helped Delia to get Ginny to stand up.

The two women helped Ginny walk towards the door. In the doorway, Elsa turned back and looked at everyone in the dining room. "Delia will come back soon. I will stay with Ginny. And I will lock the bedroom door!"

*What does that mean?* wondered Stella.

Wayne came to stand next to her. "If you ride to Walford, will you please take Chantelle with you? This is not a good situation for her. Please take her away."

Stella was still holding onto Jake. "But, Wayne! I can't! Jake is so upset. I can't leave him."

"You can leave him with me," said Wayne.

"But Wayne! He doesn't know you! He's upset. I must stay with him. I must look after him."

Wayne smiled. He put his hand on Jake's arm. "Jake," he said softly. "Stella's busy. Do you want to go fishing with me?"

"Fishing?" said Jake. "I like fishing."

Wayne looked at Max. "Is it OK if I take Jake fishing?"

Max nodded. "Sure Wayne."

*Why is Max in charge?* Stella felt angry. Then she thought. *Chris is not here, and I can't control these people. Why did Chris go away? Why hasn't he come back?*

"I'll go and find Chantelle," she said. "We will leave as soon as we can."

"Thank you," said Wayne. He took Jake's hand. "Fishing!" he said. "We'll find some food in the kitchen and go fishing."

"OK," said Jake. Wayne took him away. Stella was surprised. I thought Jake would only talk to Chris and me. But now I know that Jake trusts Chantelle. Chantelle likes him. And Jake is happy to go with Wayne.

Max looked at the clock on the wall. It was 7:00am. "Stella, it's important that you and Chantelle leave as soon as possible. We need help."

"OK. Yes." Stella hurried out of the dining room. She ran to her room and changed into horse riding clothes. She took a backpack to the kitchen, and packed some water and food for the long journey. Then she went to look for Chantelle.

## 10. THE RIDE

She found Chantelle sitting on the floor in the laundry.

"Chantelle," said Stella quietly. "Do you want to ride with me? We have to hurry."

"Yes," said Chantelle. "I can go now."

The horses were in the field next to the stables.

*How long will it take us to catch them?* wondered Stella. But Chantelle walked into the field and whistled. Both horses walked towards her. Chantelle took their halters and walked towards Stella. "I'll saddle Nero, if you can saddle Dancer," she said.

As they saddled the horses, Stella said, "Chris told me you never went riding. He said you stayed here and used your Smartphone and iPad. But the horses know you. I don't understand."

Chantelle looked sad. "The horses are my friends. Chris is my friend."

"But can you ride?" asked Stella.

Chantelle took a hair-tie from her wrist and tied up her hair. "Of course! I grew up on a farm. My mother put me on a horse before I could walk!"

"Angela?" Stella was surprised.

"Angela is not my mother!" Chantelle shouted

"Uh, OK."

Chantelle calmed down. "Listen! Wayne is my mother's brother. Last year my parents were killed in a road crash. I survived. Wayne is a computer geek. He lives in little rooms with computers. He doesn't know anything about people. Then, he suddenly found out that he had a teenager to look after. He panicked. He didn't know what to do with me. He thought I needed a woman in my life. He found Angela online. She was very clever. She said nice things in the emails, and Wayne, poor idiot, believed her. He believed he was giving me a mother. But what I got, and Wayne got, was a witch!"

Stella thought, *OK, I think I understand.*

"But why did you come here?"

"Poor Wayne. He knows that giving me 'a mother' was a big mistake. He thought that coming here would be nice for me. I could have open spaces and horses."

The horses were saddled. "Oh Chantelle. I understand. But Wayne is so good with Jake. I think he is a people person!"

"Wayne understands people like Jake very well. He doesn't understand normal people at all!"

Chantelle stroked Nero, and climbed onto his back. Stella got onto Dancer and they rode out onto the narrow road towards Walford.

Stella watched Chantelle as they rode away from Blair House and over the hills.

*She is a good horsewoman,* she thought.

They could not talk while they were riding, but after 45 minutes, they reached the top of the hill. They looked down into the valley and stopped. The bridge over Blairglen River had disappeared.

The river flowed down to the sea, and to their right it disappeared between steep hills. They could see where the bridge had been, but the deck had gone. There was no way they could cross the river.

Chantelle brought Nero close to Stella. "The bridge has gone," she said. "Can we find another bridge uphill?"

"No," said Stella. "This is the only bridge. I'm sorry. We must go back."

They turned the horses, and rode back towards Blair House.

*The bridge must have come down in the storm. At least I know why Chris hasn't come back. What can we do? We're trapped here. There is no way out.*

Back in the stable area, Stella and Chantelle unsaddled the horses.

"You said Wayne is a computer expert," Stella said to Chantelle. "Do you think he knows anything about cell towers? Maybe he can fix ours."

"I don't know," answered Chantelle. "I guess we can ask him."

"And Chantelle, can I ask a question?"

"OK. What do you want to know?"

"Why did you tell Angela you were going riding every day, and then not go? I can see you love horses, and you are a very good rider."

Chantelle hid her face behind Nero as she brushed him down. "I haven't been riding since my mother died. It makes me think of her, and that makes me sad. I did it today because my mother believed in doing the right thing. I thought she would want me to do it. But until today, the horse riding thing was just a good way of getting out of the hotel and away from Angela."

"And another question." Stella wanted to make sense of all the mysteries. Someone had killed Amy, and Stella felt she didn't know anything about these people. She didn't know who to trust.

"Wayne knows nothing about fishing. What does he do every day when he says he's going fishing?"

Chantelle laughed. "He has a computer in his fishing bag. He goes somewhere and plays with his computer. He is designing apps. A lot of the time he doesn't need an Internet connection for that."

"But he could do that in the hotel!"

"But Angela is there all the time! He is doing the same as me! Hiding from Angela."

"Wayne was going to take Jake fishing!" Stella was very frightened. *Maybe Wayne is the murderer! If I can't do anything else, at least I can protect Jake.*

Chantelle was leading Nero back out to the horse paddock. She turned back and smiled. "I guess they are somewhere with Jake's PlayStation. Don't worry."

## 11. MORE QUESTIONS THAN ANSWERS

Chantelle and Stella walked back to Blair House.

They walked down the opposite side of the house to where Amy's body lay covered by a sheet. Neither of them wanted to go near it.

They walked in the front door and stopped. Stella didn't know where to go. This was her house, but it didn't feel like her home any more. Chantelle and Stella stood in the front hall. Gilbert appeared from the dining room. "Stella! Chantelle! Why are you here?"

"The bridge has been washed away by the storm," said Stella. "We can't get to Walford. We can't talk to the police. We can't get help. We're trapped here."

"Come in here," said Gilbert. "Max will want to talk to you."

"I'll go to my room," said Chantelle.

"No," said Gilbert. "You must not be alone. Delia is in the kitchen. Why don't you go and sit with her? She will make some food for you. And don't go outside, or anywhere else, alone."

Gilbert and Stella watched Chantelle walk away. Then in the dining room, he said to Max, "The bridge was destroyed in the storm. There's no way out, and no way to communicate with anyone. We're on our own."

Max looked up from some papers he was reading, and frowned.

"OK. Stella, please sit down. I must talk to you."

Stella sat facing Max across the table. Gilbert sat next to Max. The two men stared at her. Stella felt very uncomfortable, and a little frightened.

*This is very serious,* she thought. *I feel like a prisoner. But we're all prisoners. We have no way of escaping, and someone here murdered Amy.*

Max started talking. "I am a retired policeman," he said. "Sometimes I still do jobs for the police. That is why I have been staying here.

"Drugs are getting into the country. The police believe that boats come here from Asia. They heard there was a plan to bring the drugs onto land somewhere along this part of the coast. North of Walford, there are more people and many boats. But south of Walford, the coast is very wild. The area around this hotel is the only place where it is possible to bring a boat close to land.

"No one can get here without coming across the bridge and along the road. The road ends here. Someone would notice any strange car or van. Someone would see any strangers.

"Have you ever seen another car or van here? Have you ever seen anyone who wasn't a guest?"

Stella was puzzled. "No. Never."

"But you are often inside. You are often in the kitchen at the back of the house. Could a vehicle come to the hotel without you hearing it?"

"Maybe. But I don't think so. Even if I didn't see, or hear, a strange vehicle, Chris is outside a lot. He would see or hear anything unusual. He has never said anything."

"What about a boat?" asked Gilbert. "Have you seen any boats?"

"Sometimes I see a ship far out on the ocean. But I've never seen any boats near to the beach."

"The house faces northwest," said Gilbert. You can only see the ocean in one direction. But from the orchard and the vegetable garden, you can see in every direction. And Chris is often along the coast entertaining the guests."

"But he has never said anything!" Stella was very worried.

"Why did Chris go away?" asked Max. "He left very suddenly."

"He…he got an email. He was very upset. He didn't tell me what was in it. But he packed his city clothes. He said he was going to Auckland. He said he would come back yesterday. He promised to explain everything then."

"You have no idea who the letter was from?"

"No." Stella felt her face go red. "I was so worried when Chris didn't come back. I looked at his emails. There was nothing. I think he deleted the message."

"Stella," said Max. He was very serious. "Do you think Chris got a message telling him who I really am? A retired policeman, who was staying here to watch out for drug smugglers? Maybe, Chris got that information and ran away."

"No! No! Chris would never do that! He would never have anything to do with drugs! He would never leave Jake! He would never leave me!"

"But it's very strange isn't it? Why did he leave in the middle of the night? Why hasn't he come back?"

Stella was angry. "The bridge was down! He couldn't come back!"

"We don't know when the bridge was washed away," said Gilbert.

"Who are you?" shouted Stella. "What are you doing here? Who said you could ask questions, and say terrible things about my husband?"

"Gilbert used to work on an ambulance. He recognized me, because he had seen me at crime scenes," said Max.

"Max told everyone he was a retired government worker," said Gilbert. "I guessed he didn't want anyone to know that he used to be a policeman. So I didn't say anything. I didn't know he was actually working."

"Spying!" Stella was still very angry.

"I asked Gilbert to help me. It is very difficult. Someone killed Amy. Someone who is in this house."

"Well it wasn't Chris was it? He wasn't here!"

"He might have been working with one of the guests," said Max quietly.

Stella stood up. "This is enough! I won't listen to any more!"

She walked towards the door. Then Max said quietly, "Stop, Stella. Please come back. You can help us." Stella stopped and turned back towards Max and Gilbert. She was crying.

"Why would I help you? You are saying terrible things about my husband! I don't know where Jake is! I must look after him! And Chantelle!"

"Stella, please. You can help us. We can't call the police. Amy is dead. We must try to understand everything." Max walked over to Stella. He took her arm. "Come back. Sit down. Help us."

## 12. TELL ME ABOUT THE GUESTS

Stella walked back and sat down at the table. "How can I help?" She was very angry and very frightened, but she thought, *Max and Gilbert think Chris has something to do with drugs. It's not true. If I help them, maybe I can help Chris.*

Max smiled at Stella. "I am trusting you. I believe you know nothing about the drugs or the murder. If you want to help Chris, you must tell me everything you know."

"But I don't know anything!"

"Stella. This is your hotel. You see all the guests. You know more than you think you do."

Max looked at the papers on the table. "I made a list. The guests were Amy and Ginny, Wayne, Angela and Chantelle, Gilbert and Delia, Elsa and Lou."

"And you," said Stella.

"And me," said Max, smiling. "I asked everyone what they did last night. Everyone had a story. It seems that no one killed Amy. But she is dead. One person's story is not true. But I don't know which one. So, you have to help me.

"What do you think about these people?" asked Max.

Stella thought about Max's question. She answered slowly. "Usually, I understand why people come here. They have a hobby. They like nature and outdoor activities. But this week, it was strange."

She looked at Gilbert. "Why are you here? You don't go outside. You are only interested in eating and drinking wine. There is much better food and wine in the city."

Gilbert looked at Max. Max nodded. "Tell Stella," he said.

"Delia and I have been married for a long time. I worked for the ambulance service. Delia was a nurse in the emergency room at the hospital. Then a month ago, we won a lottery. Now we have a lot of money. We thought it was wonderful. Now we will never need to work again. But many people knew we had won the lottery. People came to our house. People wanted our money. It was very hard. We came here to escape."

"Now I understand," said Stella.

"What do you think about Ginny and Amy?" asked Max.

"Uh. I think they were friends. They liked birdwatching. I didn't think it was strange that they were here."

"But watching birds is a good reason to be along the coast. Maybe they were waiting for the drug delivery," said Max.

"Maybe," answered Stella.

"And then there is Wayne, Angela and Chantelle," said Max. "I don't understand them. Why are they here?"

Stella felt uncomfortable. *I know why they are here but I don't want to say. Chantelle told me, but maybe it is a secret.*

Max was watching Stella. *She knows, but she doesn't want to say,* he thought.

"Stella," he said. "Chantelle is very young. I know you want to protect her. But the best way to help her is to tell us what you know."

Stella didn't talk for a long time. Then, she said, "Chantelle's parents died. Wayne is her uncle. He wanted to give Chantelle a good life. He has no experience as a parent. He went online and found Angela. He married her because he wanted to give Chantelle a mother. It was a bad idea."

"But why are they here?" asked Max.

"Wayne knows his marriage to Angela was a mistake. He knows Chantelle is very unhappy. Chantelle lived on a farm with her parents. He told Angela they must come here, so that Chantelle could have open air and horse riding. I don't think it has anything to do with drugs."

Max and Gilbert smiled at each other. "That's good!" said Gilbert.

"What do you mean?" asked Stella.

The door to the dining room opened, and Wayne and Jake walked in.

"What did you find?" Max asked Wayne.

"We did what you asked. We went up to the cell tower," said Wayne. "Your guess was right. The cell tower did not fall down in the wind. Someone cut it down."

"Can you fix it?" asked Gilbert.

"I'd like to help, but I'm a computer expert, not an engineer," answered Wayne.

"Boat," said Jake. He looked very happy. "There is a boat!"

No one listened to him.

"Come on Jake," said Wayne. "We need food. Let's go to the kitchen." After they left the room, Max was talking, "I agree with you. I don't think Chantelle or Wayne have anything to do with drugs, or anything to do with Amy's murder.

"Ginny, Angela, Elsa, Lou. Who killed Amy? And why?"

"Do you think Ginny killed Amy?" asked Stella.

Max shrugged. "I don't know. Ginny is in Delia and Gilbert's room with Elsa. Delia gave Ginny a sleeping tablet. After she left the room, Elsa locked the door. The two women are still in there, and Elsa won't open the door."

"Where is Angela?" Stella was very confused.

Gilbert answered. "She's in the bar with Lou. She has been drinking since you left."

Stella looked at the clock. "But it's only ten thirty am! She and Lou are drinking already?"

"Lou's not drinking. Angela took a bottle of whisky from the bar. I think she has drunk about half of it. Lou is playing solitaire."

"Stella," said Max. "We know that Amy and Ginny were in their bedroom at five thirty pm yesterday. Where was everyone yesterday from breakfast until then?"

Stella tried to remember. "Everyone was at breakfast. Then Wayne, Lou, Amy and Ginny asked for picnic lunches. I made the lunch boxes and put them on the table in the front hall. I didn't see anyone go out, but the lunches were gone by ten o'clock.

"I saw Wayne, Amy and Ginny came back in the middle of the afternoon before the rain started. They went to their rooms, I think.

"I didn't see Lou from breakfast time until I came into the bar with the snacks. That was also the first time I had seen Elsa since breakfast. Gilbert and Delia were in the guest lounge most of the day. Well, when they weren't in the dining room."

Gilbert smiled. "We came here to get away from all the stress. We are both very tired, and just want to relax."

"Where were you, Max?" asked Stella. "I saw you at breakfast. The next time I saw you, was upstairs about five thirty pm."

"I got a message two days ago. It said that the drugs would probably be delivered in the next thirty-six hours. The police know someone in Auckland is expecting a delivery about now. I thought the boat would come at night. I went outside and watched all night. Nothing happened. So after breakfast, I went upstairs to sleep. I slept almost all day. Last night, I watched from midnight until four am. Again, there was nothing. I am sure there is a connection between the drug delivery and Amy's murder."

"Amy and Ginny had a big fight," said Gilbert. "Maybe it has nothing to do with the drugs. Maybe Ginny lost control and killed her friend."

"Maybe," said Max. "There is only one way to find out. We must make Elsa open the door, and we must talk to Ginny. Stella, please come with me. I think Elsa will open the door if you speak to her."

"OK," said Stella. "I will try."

"Gilbert. Everyone else is downstairs. Please stay here and watch. Please try to keep everyone safe."

"OK," said Gilbert. "I will do my best. But it would be much easier if I knew who to protect, and who should be locked up."

## 13. GINNY'S STORY

Upstairs, Stella knocked on the door of the locked bedroom. "Elsa! Open the door," she called. "I must talk to Ginny."

"No!" shouted Elsa. "I'm frightened. Ginny is frightened. We're not coming out!"

"Well, can Max and I come in? He is a policeman. He will keep you safe. It is very important. Please! I want to help you."

"No!"

"If you don't open the door, I will break it down!" shouted Max. "Someone in this house murdered Amy. I must find out who did it, and I can't do that if Ginny won't talk to me!"

The door suddenly opened. Elsa moved away, and they saw Ginny lying on the bed.

She looked terrible. Her face was so white, she looked like a ghost. Elsa moved to the bed, and lifted Ginny into a sitting position. She pushed pillows behind her.

"I think maybe we should talk to Stella and Max," she said to Ginny. "I'll get you some water."

Elsa brought a glass of water, and helped Ginny to drink. Then she climbed onto the bed next to Ginny. The two women stared at Max and Stella, and waited.

Max turned and locked the door. He sat down on the sofa, and waved to Stella to sit next to him. Stella thought it was strange. *After all that shouting, now he doesn't seem to be in a hurry.*

There was silence for a while, and then Ginny started to speak.

"I must tell you why Amy and I had a fight. I knew Amy many

years ago. We went to high school together. She was a lovely person, and we were very good friends. But after high school everything went wrong for her. She had a hard life, and she started taking drugs. I went to college and got a job with a wildlife sanctuary. I didn't see her for almost fifteen years. Then, two years ago, I saw her in New York. She was on the street asking people for money. Her situation was very bad. I wanted to help her. I wanted to save her.

"I took her to the wildlife sanctuary. It was very difficult for her to give up the drugs, but finally, she was successful. Her health recovered, and I started to see the person she used to be. I promised her, that when she had not taken drugs for one year, we would take a trip. We would travel. I gave up my job, and we came to this country. In the beginning, it was very good. My specialty is birds. We stayed in different places and went birdwatching. Amy was healthy and happy. She was becoming interested in birds. Then I fell and broke my ankle. I had to stay in a hospital in Auckland. I was in hospital for ten days. I worried because Amy was alone in the city. I wasn't there to look after her.

"When I left the hospital, Amy and I stayed in Auckland for a month, until I could walk well. Amy seemed different. I didn't know why, but she was very quiet, and didn't talk to me.

"Then she told me she wanted to come to this hotel. She said the birds were wonderful. It was a place she wanted to visit. I was so happy that Amy had found a birdwatching place."

Ginny's eyes filled with tears and she couldn't speak. Elsa gave her some more water, and finally Ginny started talking again.

"We came here. Amy was right. It is a great place to study birds. But Amy didn't want to go out. It was difficult to persuade her to go out. I didn't know why. Then yesterday, I understood everything. It was cold when we came back here. Amy went to have a shower. I went into the bathroom to talk to her. She was taking drugs.

"I forced her to talk to me. She told me the sad story. While I was in hospital, Amy was lonely. She went out to bars. She got drunk. She talked a lot. She met a guy, but she was so drunk she couldn't remember anything about him. When she got back to the hotel, she found drugs in her bag. I guess the guy put them there. Poor Amy. I wasn't there to look after her. She was not strong enough.

"She wouldn't tell me any more, but later that night she told me the rest of the story. She started getting messages on her phone.

Someone told her to come here. They promised more drugs. The drug gang wanted information about this place. We came last week, and Amy has been sending information about this hotel every day."

"What kind of information?" Stella was angry and confused.

"They wanted to know about the people who lived here. They wanted to know where people went, and at what times of the day. It's all on her mobile phone."

"Who was she sending the information to?" asked Max. "Where is her mobile phone now? When Gilbert and I searched your room, we didn't find it."

Ginny sighed. "I took it from her when I went downstairs. I told her what she was doing was wrong, and she couldn't send any more messages." She put her hand under the pillows and pulled out the phone. Max walked across to the bed and took it from her.

He looked at the text messages. "The address is just a string of numbers and letters, and we can't find out who it belongs to. Thank you, Ginny. I know this is difficult for you. Maybe you should eat and drink something, and try to get some sleep. Stella or Delia will make some food for you. When we leave, lock the door again. Don't open the door to anyone except Delia, Stella, Gilbert or me."

He put the phone in his pocket and turned to leave the room.

"Wait," said Elsa. "I have something to tell you too."

## 14. ELSA'S STORY

"I work in a bar in Auckland. It's a very nice bar. The drinks are expensive and it is mostly business people who go there. I like my job, but I'm getting older, and I get very tired.

"A man came to the bar a few times. He always talked to me and gave me very good tips. He took me out to dinner once. Then one night he asked me if I ever took a vacation. He would like to take me on a vacation. I was very happy. I thought he liked me. I was married once, many years ago, but since then, I have been alone. I said, 'yes'.

"He didn't tell me where we were going. He said it was a surprise. I thought maybe we would go to Sydney, or on a cruise. I didn't see him again for a week. I thought it was strange. But he said he was a businessman, so I thought he was busy. Then the day before we were going to leave, he came to the bar very late. He told me we were coming here! It didn't seem like the kind of place he would like, but I was so happy to be going away with him, I didn't ask any questions.

"On the way to Walford, he told me I must pretend to be his wife. He said he didn't want people talking about me. He said that he was in the middle of a big deal, and he needed to go somewhere quiet. Some place where he could get away from people. He didn't want people contacting him. That was why he was using a different name. We were going to be Mr and Mrs Cottingville.

"It was OK when we arrived. But after lunch, we went to our room. Lou spent all afternoon sending texts, and waiting for answers. I asked him if we could go for a walk, but he said he was busy. He seemed to be angry and stressed. I thought it must be something about this big business deal. But it was strange, because he had said he wanted to get away from his work for a while.

"I sat on our balcony and read a book. Then about six pm, he came onto the balcony. He told me we were going down to the bar. He seemed pleased. His mood was much better.

"Down in the bar, I drank too much. Usually I don't drink at all, but I knew I had made a terrible mistake coming here with him. I didn't know anything about him, and he was making me nervous. He talked to everyone else, but he didn't talk to me. I thought he was watching me. I didn't want to say anything wrong. I was drunk, and I was worried I would say I was not his wife, and our name wasn't Cottingville. So I didn't talk at all.

"When we went upstairs, I fell asleep immediately. The next morning he seemed excited. I was surprised when he said he was going out all day for a walk. I wanted to go with him. We went upstairs, and while he was putting on walking shoes and putting things in a backpack, I said I would go with him. He suddenly got very angry. He held my arms and shouted at me. He pushed me to the ground. When I got up, he had left the room, and I heard the key turn in the lock. I was locked in our bedroom! I stayed there all day. I heard you Stella, when you came to the door about five thirty pm, but I didn't answer. I was too embarrassed. I had been so stupid!

"It was about six pm when Lou came back. He was very wet and dirty, but he seemed pleased. He was so nice to me. He said 'sorry' many times. He said his bad behaviour was because of stress. He said we would go downstairs, and have a lovely party. He took a shower, and then we went down to the bar. I didn't believe he was sorry. I was frightened of him, but I went to the bar, because I thought it would be a mistake to make him angry. I thought he might hurt me again."

Elsa pulled up the sleeves of the loose shirt she was wearing. Stella was shocked. Elsa's arms were covered in red marks.

Before Stella or Max could say anything, Elsa started talking again.

"I was very careful not to drink too much. Lou said many times, 'Have another drink. Enjoy yourself.' He brought me a lot of drinks, but I poured them into plant pots." Elsa smiled a little. "I'm sorry, Stella. I think your beautiful houseplants will die.

"I pretended to be drunk. When we went back to our room, I lay down. I pretended to be asleep. After a while, I did go to sleep. I don't know what happened in the night. But I am frightened of Lou. I want to stay in this room. I will look after Ginny."

Stella walked across to Elsa and hugged her. "Oh, Elsa! I am so sorry. Lou was so unkind to you!"

Elsa pulled away from Stella. "Don't be sorry for me. I am a stupid, lonely woman. Please go away."

"I am a stupid, lonely woman, too!" said Ginny. "We will look after each other. Now, please leave."

Stella and Max went out of the room, but Max turned in the doorway and said. "You are both very brave women. Thank you for telling me your stories, and please, lock the door!"

## 15. I SAW A BOAT

Max and Stella waited outside the door until they heard the key turn in lock.

"So Lou is the drug smuggler, and the murderer!" said Stella. "What are we going to do?"

"Maybe," answered Max. "He is not a nice man. But we don't know that he is the drug smuggler, or the murderer. We must be very careful. Please go and make some food for Elsa and Ginny. I will find Gilbert."

When Stella arrived at the kitchen door, she stopped and listened. She could hear people laughing. *That's Delia!* she thought. *And the other person laughing is Chantelle! This is the first time I have heard her laugh.*

But when she opened the kitchen door, the scene was very different. Delia was pointing a kitchen knife at Stella. Chantelle was standing in front of Jake. She was holding a kitchen knife too!

"Oh Stella. Sorry," said Delia relaxing and lowering her knife. "There is no lock on this door. We have been thinking someone will attack us. Come in!"

Stella walked into the kitchen and sat down next to Jake. "I don't understand," she said. "I heard you laughing. Then I walk in, and you are ready to attack me with a knife."

"I have worked as an emergency department nurse for many years. You learn to relax when you can. And Chantelle is only fifteen years old, but she knows stress as well. Her life has been very difficult. But we have a problem. Gilbert told us not to leave the kitchen. He said we must not go outside. But Jake is talking about a boat. He wants to go outside and look at the boat."

A boat! thought Stella. Is this the boat bringing drugs here?

"Jake. Did you see a boat?"

"Yes. I saw a boat," said Jake.

"When did you see the boat?"

Jake didn't answer. Stella held his hands and forced him to look at her.

"Jake. When did you see the boat?"

Jake looked confused. "I don't know." He turned away from Stella, and looked out the kitchen window.

"Max wants some food to take up to Elsa and Ginny," Stella told Delia.

"Did Elsa open the door? Did you talk to them?"

"Yes. It was very sad. They are both very unhappy."

"Well. Chantelle and I have been making sandwiches. I think we have made too many, but we didn't have anything else to do," said Delia.

Stella laughed. "Yes! You have made a lot. But it was a good idea. Can we make coffee, and put sandwiches on a tray for Elsa and Ginny?"

Jake was still staring out the window, when Stella picked up the tray to take upstairs.

"Uh, Stella," said Delia. "I don't think you should go alone. Gilbert told us not to leave the kitchen."

"Yes," said Stella. "But didn't he mean, 'don't go outside'?"

"Maybe," said Delia, "but I will be happier if you take Jake with you."

"OK," said Stella. "Jake. Please carry this tray for me."

Jake looked away from the window and stood up. He picked up the tray, and followed Stella upstairs.

Elsa opened the door as soon as Stella called out. "Thank you," she smiled. She took the tray and closed the door. Stella heard the key turn. As Stella and Jake went back to the kitchen, Jake said. "I saw a boat."

"Yes Jake," said Stella. "But you can't go out to look at the boat. Not today."

"I saw Chris," said Jake smiling. "I saw a big boat. Not a kayak. Chris will take me fishing."

Stella felt very cold. She stopped and put her hand on Jake's arm.

*Oh no! Did Jake see a boat on the day of the storm? Did Chris come here? Did Chris come here with drugs?*

"Jake! When did you see the boat? When did you see Chris?" Stella was very frightened.

"I saw the boat when I was on the hill."

Stella's mind was racing. *Jake was with me all morning and at lunchtime, yesterday. But then I didn't see him again for about two hours. I didn't see him until the weather got bad. Did he go out along the coast and see Chris come here on a boat? I must be very careful.*

Stella wanted to shout and scream, but she forced herself to talk very slowly and quietly. "Jake. You must not tell anyone you saw Chris. It's a secret."

Jake nodded. "Chris said it was a secret."

"You talked to Chris!"

Jake looked worried. "I wanted to talk to Chris. I wanted to say hello. But Chris… Chris…" He couldn't explain, but shook his head and put his finger on his lips.

Stella understood. Jake had seen Chris, but Chris had signalled to Jake to be quiet.

"It's OK, Jake. I understand. It's a secret."

"Yes Stella. It's a secret," he smiled.

Back in the kitchen, Gilbert and Max had joined Chantelle and Delia. They were sitting at the table eating sandwiches. Max was telling them what Ginny and Elsa had said.

"Are Elsa and Ginny OK?" asked Max.

"I think so," she answered. "Sit down," she said to Jake. "Chantelle will give you some sandwiches and coke."

"Delia told us that Jake saw a boat," said Gilbert.

"Yes. He saw a boat." answered Stella. She was very frightened. *I must be very careful. I must make sure they don't know Chris was here.*

"Can I ask Jake some questions?" asked Max. "I want to know when he saw the boat."

"Please understand," said Stella. "Jake remembers some things very well. In some ways, he is very clever. He can play his computer games very well. But he has no idea about time. For Jake, everything is now. He will talk about something that happened, but he won't know if it was this morning, yesterday, or a week ago."

"OK," said Max. "There are too many people in this room. Why don't we go to the dining room?"

Stella took a plate of sandwiches and a glass of coke from Chantelle. "Come on, Jake," she said. "We'll go to the dining room."

As she left the room, Stella asked Gilbert, "Where are Angela and Lou?"

"Angela drank half a bottle of whisky," said Gilbert. "She is asleep in the guest lounge. Wayne said it was better to leave her."

Stella looked at Wayne. "Yes," he said. "If we wake her up, she'll start screaming about being trapped, and being murdered. Let her sleep."

"And Lou?"

Delia looked angry. "He came in here, and took sandwiches and coffee. I think he went back to the bar. I guess he is still playing solitaire."

## 16. A FACE AT THE WINDOW

They were walking into the dining room when there was a scream from the guest lounge. Max ran towards the sound. Stella and Jake ran after him.

Angela was standing in the middle of the room. She was pointing at the window. "A man! There was a man at the window! He's come to kill me!"

Everyone came running from the kitchen as well. Max hurried to the window and looked out. He said something, but no one could hear him because Angela was making so much noise.

"Angela, calm down," said Gilbert. "I'm sure you imagined the man at the window."

Angela didn't stop screaming. "Help me. Save me! There was a man outside the window!" Chantelle walked over to Angela, and hit her very hard in the face. It made no difference. Chantelle sighed, took the glass of coke that Stella was still holding, and threw the coke into Angela's face. The screaming stopped, but Angela started crying noisily.

Delia and Gilbert pulled Angela into a chair. "So, there has been someone else here. Someone we didn't know about," Gilbert looked pleased.

It took a few minutes for Angela to calm down enough to answer questions.

"Tell us what you saw," said Max.

"I was asleep on the sofa. I woke up. There was a face at the window. I am so frightened!"

"Who was it?" asked Max.

"A man. I don't know who it was."

Stella looked around the room. Chantelle was sitting on one of the sofas with Jake. Jake had a cushion over his face. Delia and Gilbert were standing behind Angela's chair. Max was still by the window. Stella didn't believe that some other person had been around Blair House since yesterday.

"Lou," said Stella loudly. "Where is Lou? He must have heard all the noise. Where is he?"

Chantelle looked into the bar. "He's not here."

"And Wayne? Where is Wayne? Who was the man at the window? Was it Lou? Was it Wayne?"

"It was me," said a voice behind her. Stella was amazed. Chris's voice! Chris was standing in the doorway. "I'm sorry I frightened Angela when I looked in the window."

"Chris!" Stella could not believe her eyes.

"Hi Chris!" said Jake from the sofa. "Is it a secret?"

Chris smiled at Jake. "No mate. It's not a secret now."

Gilbert walked across to the door and stood with his hand on Chris's shoulder. Stella hurried towards them. She was still very worried and frightened. *I am so pleased to see him. But how did he get here? Has he been here all the time? Gilbert thinks Chris might have something to do with Amy's murder, and the drugs. He is making sure Chris can't escape.*

Chris took Stella's hand. He looked very tired. Stella looked into his face. *I know my husband. He hasn't done anything wrong!*

"Chris. Will you come into the dining room? Gilbert, please stay here and look after everyone else," said Max.

Gilbert nodded. Chris and Max walked towards the dining room. Stella followed them. "Stella. Stay in the guest lounge with the others, please."

"No!" Stella was angry. She glared at Max. "Chris doesn't know anything about what has been happening here! You will try to trick him. This is my house, and my husband! I'm coming with you! And before you say one word to him, he is going to have a cup of coffee and something to eat!"

Max shrugged. "OK. So why don't we all go to the kitchen?"

## 17. CHRIS'S STORY

The kitchen table was a mess. There were half-eaten sandwiches and half-filled cups of coffee. Everyone had jumped up and run into the lounge when they heard Angela screaming.

Stella cleared a space at one end of the table. She poured coffee for Chris and put some sandwiches in front of him.

She sat down next to Chris and glared across the table at Max who smiled at her. "Can I start now?"

"OK Chris," said Max. " You have a lot to explain. Why are you here? How did you get here? When did you come back from Auckland?"

Chris didn't answer Max's questions.

"What's going on? Why are you in charge? You sound like a policeman."

"Chris," Stella squeezed his hand. "Max is a retired policeman. He was staying here because he was doing a job for the police. Amy's dead. She was murdered last night. Someone had to take control."

"Amy's dead! This is worse than I thought." Chris was shocked. "I saw Delia, Gilbert, Chantelle, Angela and Jake in the lounge. Where are Elsa and Ginny? Are they OK?"

*He didn't ask about Wayne and Lou,* thought Stella. *Does he know where they are?*

"Ginny and Elsa are OK. They have locked themselves in Delia and Gilbert's bedroom," explained Stella.

"But why?" Chris was becoming more worried, and more confused.

Max was getting frustrated. "Stella can tell you everything later, Chris! Start talking please!"

"I don't know where to start," said Chris.

"Tell us why you went to Auckland," said Max grimly.

Stella felt sick. Max still thinks Chris has something to do with the drugs!

"I don't want to tell you," said Chris. "I didn't tell Stella, and it's private."

"Chris," said Stella. "It's OK. Terrible things have happened here. No one knows who to believe. We can't have secrets. Please tell him."

Chris sighed and rubbed his eyes. "OK. My family owned this house. They were not rich, but there was still quite a lot of money. When our parents died, this house, and twenty-five percent of the money became mine. The rest of the money was for Jake. Jake does not understand many things about life. He doesn't understand money. So the money was put in a trust for him. The family lawyer and I control the trust together. I got a letter from the family lawyer. He said someone had told the police that I was stealing money from Jake's trust. He said the police would investigate. While they were checking, the police planned to stop all activity on Stella's and my bank accounts. They planned to take control of Jake's trust fund. And the worst thing was, they planned to take Jake away from here. They planned to put him in a special home for people like him.

"I love my brother. This is a good place for him to live. I would never touch his money. I had to stop them from taking him away. I had to go to Auckland to fix the problem."

He turned to Stella. "I'm sorry. I didn't want you to worry."

"Oh, Chris," sighed Stella.

"I went to Auckland, and spent many hours talking to policemen and the family lawyer. It was easy to prove I had done nothing wrong, but it took all day. Sometime during the day, I lost text and email connection with Stella. So I left Auckland as soon as I could. The weather was very bad, but I wanted to come back. When I got to the Blairglen River, the bridge was gone. I was so close, but I had to go back.

"I drove back to Walford. It was late. I couldn't find anyone to help me. I borrowed a motor launch this morning. I wanted to get here as soon as I could. The bridge has gone. There is no way to bring guests here, or to take them back. We have the old jetty next to the boatshed. I thought the launch would be useful."

"So, when did you arrive?" Max asked.

"I came this morning. I arrived about ten thirty. When I was coming into the beach, I saw the cell tower had disappeared. I thought it must have fallen over in the storm.

"I'm sorry, Stella. I thought it was only storm damage. I decided to go and look at the cell tower first. If I could fix it, then one problem would be solved. I climbed up the hill. The cell tower didn't fall down in the storm. It was cut down."

"We know that," said Max. "Wayne and Jake went to look at it."

Chris shrugged. "I went to get tools and rope from the boatshed. The cell tower had been cut down. So I knew something was wrong. I thought if I could fix the tower, I could call the police.

"Then I saw that all the kayaks in the boatshed had holes in them. I was very worried about you and Jake." Chris put his arms around Stella. "I didn't know what to do. I knew I must be very careful. I wanted to see you. I wanted to know you were safe. But I thought it might be dangerous for you if I came to the house.

"I wanted to find out what was happening. A little while ago, I looked in the kitchen window, but Jake saw me. I signalled to Jake 'don't say anything'."

"Jake said it was a secret!" said Stella. "But I didn't know when he saw you. I didn't understand. I was so stressed. I didn't listen."

"Then I went to look in the guest lounge window," Chris continued. "Angela saw me, and started screaming."

Max listened very carefully to everything that Chris said.

But Stella was surprised by his next question. "Who told the police you were stealing Jake's money?"

"The police don't know. It was an anonymous message. But there was a lot of information in the message. It seemed like someone knew a lot about the people in this hotel," answered Chris. "There were photographs too. That's why they thought it might be true. The police are always very careful when someone like Jake is involved. They wanted to protect him. They didn't know it was all lies."

"Amy...," said Max.

Stella understood Max's meaning. "Did Amy send the message to the police?" she asked Max.

"No. I don't think so. But Amy gave someone a lot of

information. Someone wanted to know how the hotel worked, and who might see a boat or a vehicle coming here," said Max.

## 18. MAX'S IDEAS

"I think I understand some of the story. Chris is usually outside during the day. He is working in the garden or the orchard. Sometimes he is organizing activities for guests. He would see anything strange; a car coming from Walford; a boat coming to the beach. Chris would see everything. Someone wanted to make him leave here. It was very clever. If Chris was away, there was almost no one who would see a boat coming here. Maybe one of the guests would see a boat but they would not think so much about it. Someone thought of a way to force Chris to go to Auckland."

"But who?" asked Chris. "It was a lot of work to get me away from here. Why was it so important? And why did someone destroy the cell tower and kayaks? It doesn't make sense."

"Oh, I think it does," said Max grimly. "A drug delivery, worth maybe millions of dollars, was to be delivered by boat. It's worth a lot of trouble and a lot of planning, for so much money. I guess the plan was for the delivery to be made yesterday. That's why you got the email the night before. The email that sent you rushing off to Auckland.

"This is what I think happened. The plan to deliver the drugs here was made a few weeks ago. Amy met someone from the gang in a bar. She talked about her friend Ginny and the birdwatching. They gave her drugs, and promised more if she came here and sent them information.

"The safest time to deliver the drugs was very early in the morning. Maybe they were buried on the beach, or hidden somewhere close to the beach. Then I told everyone a storm was coming. Sometime before the weather got bad, the gang member who was staying here at the hotel went out to get the drugs and hide them somewhere safer. We know that Amy, Ginny, Wayne and Lou were all out along the coast during that time. One of them moved the drugs.

"But I think someone else saw the drugs being moved. To be safe, the cell tower was destroyed. That meant that no one could telephone the police, or send an email message about what they had seen. To be extra safe, the kayaks and mountain bikes were also destroyed."

"And the four-wheel motor bike," said Stella.

"No. I think that was done later. I think the gangster planned to use the motorbike to take the drugs to the bridge. A car would be waiting there, and the gangster could either escape with the drugs, or come back here and pretend to be a normal guest for a few days."

"Oh," said Stella. "But when they got to the bridge, it had been destroyed by the storm. So they had to come back. But where are the drugs now? And why damage the bike so it couldn't be used?"

Max shrugged. "I don't know. But there must be a reason."

Chris was staring around the room. "This is terrible. But who murdered Amy, and why?"

"I can only guess," answered Max. "But, say it was Amy who saw the drugs being moved. She has been a drug addict for many years, so it might have been easy for her to guess what they were. Did she go and take some of the drugs? Or did she go to the person she saw, and ask for some in exchange for her silence?

"I don't know what happened. But sometime after midnight, and before about four am this morning, someone attacked Amy. They broke her neck and threw her body off the balcony.

"The drug gang had made a very good plan. It would have been perfect, but then there was the storm. The storm meant the drugs had to be moved during the day. The cell tower and all forms of transport had to be destroyed. Then the gang member, who was staying here, couldn't escape because the bridge collapsed."

Chantelle ran into the kitchen. "Please come!"

She ran to the front door, and they followed her.

## 19. LIFE MATTERS

Wayne was lying on the steps outside the house. Delia and Gilbert were kneeling next to him. They were talking urgently to each other.

"What's happened?" asked Max.

"Get everyone inside!" said Gilbert. "Now!"

Chantelle was crying noisily. She was very frightened. She fell to the ground. Chris picked her up, and looked at Stella. "Where shall I take her?"

"Take her to our bedroom," said Stella. She turned to Jake and Angela. "Please come with me."

A few minutes later, they were all in the bedroom. It was a strange situation. Jake was sitting on the floor. Angela had come with Stella without saying a word. She was sitting at Stella's dressing table. She was pale and her lips were pinched together. She was staring at Chantelle, who was lying on the bed. But she didn't do anything to help her. Chris stood by the door.

"Can I come in?" said someone standing behind Chris. Chris and Stella jumped. It was Elsa!

"Oh Elsa," said Stella. "Did you hear all the noise? Is Ginny OK?"

"That's why I've come downstairs. I went to the guest lounge, but Max shouted at me. He told me to come here. He wouldn't listen to me. Ginny's gone."

"Gone?"

"After Ginny and I ate the food you brought up, I fell asleep. I'm sorry. I was so tired.

When I woke up, Ginny was gone."

"Where is she?" asked Stella.

"I don't know. The door was unlocked, and she was not in the bedroom or the bathroom. I am still very frightened, but I knew I must come down and tell someone. And I don't want to be alone."

"Come in, and I'll close the door," said Chris. The bedroom was crowded with so many people.

Stella sat on the bed and stared helplessly at Chris. He was standing against the closed door with his arms folded.

*Oh no!* thought Stella. *I believed everything Ginny told Max and me. But what if it was all lies? Ginny is a tall, strong woman. She could easily kill Amy. And what is wrong with Wayne?*

Stella's question was soon answered. There was a knock at the door. Chris opened the door a little, and looked out. "Can you and Stella come out and talk to me, please?" It was Max's voice.

Stella hurried out of the room and joined Chris and Max in the hallway.

"Wayne is dead," said Max. "Delia and Gilbert are professionals. They did everything they could, but they couldn't save him."

Stella's legs felt weak. She thought she would faint. But Chris put his arm around her and pulled her up. "Not now, Stella," he said.

Max was still talking. "He was shot."

"Did you talk to him?" asked Chris. "Did he tell you who shot him?"

"He talked a little. He tried very hard to tell me what happened. He felt bad about the cell tower. He went back to see if he could fix it. Then he asked us to look after Chantelle. I asked him who shot him. He couldn't answer. Maybe he didn't know. Then he died."

"Ginny has disappeared," said Chris. "Elsa came down to tell us."

It was Max's turn to be shocked. "What! I believed Ginny's story!"

"I believed her too," said Stella.

"So," said Max. "Lou and Ginny are outside somewhere. One of them is a member of a drug gang, and a murderer. Or, maybe they both are.

"Chris, I need your help. Gilbert will help me, but you are younger and stronger. Please come with us. We must find Lou, and we must find Ginny."

"No!" shouted Stella. "It's dangerous."

"Stella," said Chris. "I must help Max. I'm sorry. Can you look after Jake? Can you look after everyone here?"

"Please, Stella," said Max. "Please tell Chantelle and Angela that Wayne is dead. Please look after everyone. Delia will come and help you."

Chris hugged Stella, and walked away with Max. Stella stood at the bedroom door watching them. Soon Delia came out of the lounge, closing the door behind her. "Oh Stella!" she said. "This is awful. And now we have to tell Chantelle that Wayne is dead. Poor child. She is very strong, but this might be too much for her."

"Delia," said Stella. "Gilbert is going out with Max and Chris to find a murderer. Someone who has killed two people! Aren't you frightened?"

"Someone who has killed two people," said Delia slowly. "Stella, that's the point. Yes, it's dangerous. But lives matter. If Gilbert died, it would be the end of my world. We only have each other, but I would know that he died doing the right thing. Come on, we have to tell Chantelle and Angela what has happened."

As the men prepared to go outside, Max said, "Do you have any guns in the house?"

"Yes," said Chris. "I was thinking about that. Sometimes wild pigs come down from the hills and destroy the vegetable gardens. I have two hunting rifles. Shall we take them?"

"I think we must," said Max. "Where are they?"

"Come this way," said Chris. Max and Gilbert followed him to a room at the back of the house. It was filled with outdoor wear and old furniture. In one corner was a gun cabinet. Chris took a bunch of keys from his pocket and unlocked the cabinet. He handed two rifles to Max. "The ammunition is in the laundry. I keep it in a locked cupboard away from the rifles. I like to be careful."

A few minutes later, the men had left the house. Chris was carrying one rifle and Max, the other. "Where do you want to look?" Chris asked Max.

"I don't know where to look, but I thought we should check around the boathouse first," he answered. "What will be the best way to go? We don't want to be seen."

"OK. Follow me." Chris led the other men along a narrow path that ran between the orchard and the hill behind the house. "We can get to the vegetable garden this way. We can see the boathouse from there."

## 20. I AM ALONE

Back in the house, the situation was difficult. Chris and Stella's bedroom was full of people. Delia told Chantelle and Angela about Wayne's death. Chantelle cried and screamed, but Angela didn't react at all. She was still sitting at the dressing table, staring at nothing. Jake was on the floor in a corner of the room, hidden under a blanket.

Delia was on the bed trying to comfort Chantelle. Elsa and Stella stood at the end of the bed, staring at the heartbroken young girl.

"We can't stay in this room," said Stella. "There is nowhere to hide, and someone could shoot at us through the window. There is a corner of the dining room that is hidden from the windows. We should go there. We can turn the big side-table over and hide behind it."

Delia looked up. "Yes. Maybe that would be best. But we must all stay together."

It was a strange procession. Stella went first, leading Jake by the hand. Next came Elsa and Delia, half-carrying Chantelle, and finally Angela. They walked very close together, so they arrived at the big double doors of the dining room at the same time.

Stella opened the doors and gasped. Ginny was sitting at a table in the middle of the room pointing a pistol at them.

"Come in," she said. "Take a seat. Sit where I can see you."

Oh no! thought Stella. Chris asked me to keep everyone safe, and I have brought them straight to the killer!

"Hi, Ginny," Delia was speaking. "I'm pleased to see you. Are you OK?"

Ginny didn't answer. She waved her gun at them. Then she shouted. "Sit!"

Everyone hurried to find a chair. They sat facing Ginny and waited, watching the gun in Ginny's hand."

*Why did I believe her story? Why was I so stupid?* Stella asked herself. *She must have killed Amy. She sells drugs, and she kills people.*

"Chantelle is sad." Jake's voice sounded very loud. Everyone else turned to look at Jake, but Stella looked at Delia. She saw Delia's mouth move. 'Keep her talking!'

Stella thought, *I understand what Delia's telling me. If we can keep Ginny talking, maybe there will be enough time for the men to come back.*

"Please tell us what happened," said Stella. "I didn't realise you are a drug smuggler."

"Drug smuggler!" screamed Ginny. She pointed the gun at Stella. "I'll kill you! I hate drugs!"

"I know you are not a drug smuggler," said Delia in a very quiet voice. "Why don't you tell us what happened?"

Ginny looked pleased. "Yes. OK. I'll tell you."

"I was in your bedroom with Elsa for a long time. Elsa was very kind, but I felt restless. I wanted to get out. I wanted to be outside. I wanted fresh air. I wanted to look at birds. Elsa fell asleep. I took my walking boots. I went down the fire escape at the end of the hallway.

"I went to the orchard and sat under a tree. I thought, 'Someone from the drug gang killed Amy. But why? Amy didn't know who told her to come here. All the messages, and the promise of more drugs came by text. She couldn't tell anyone anything.

"I thought, *Something must have happened yesterday. Did Amy see something?* She came along the coast with me, but after lunch, she wanted to sit down. So I left her near the boathouse, and went to take photographs alone.

"I was sitting in the orchard thinking about Amy. I was feeling very bad. I felt sad and angry at the same time. Then I saw Wayne. He was going to the boathouse. I waited until he was inside. I looked through the window. He had opened a big box in the corner. He was looking for something. He pulled out some packages that were wrapped in plastic. I was sure they were drugs. So I was sure that he had killed Amy. So I went into the boathouse, and I shot him.

"He looked so surprised! He said, 'Ginny? Why did you shoot me?' He went out of the boatshed towards the house. He was bleeding a lot. Is he OK?"

"You put a bullet in his lung," said Delia. "I don't know how he got to the house. Gilbert and I tried to save him, but we couldn't."

"Oh Chantelle," said Ginny. "I'm sorry that I killed Wayne. It was a mistake."

"I hate you," said Chantelle.

Ginny was upset. "Chantelle, I like you. I don't want you to hate me. I think Wayne really loved you. I have made you sad, but don't worry. I will make everything better for you. It's better to be dead. So I'll kill you.

"And Elsa. Elsa doesn't know it, but she is alone like me. I think it's better to be dead. So I will kill Chantelle and Elsa. But Delia and Stella might try to stop me. So I'll kill them first."

"When did you learn to use a pistol?" asked Delia quickly. "I think you know a lot about them."

"Sometimes there were bears in the wildlife sanctuary where I worked. We all had pistols. We all learnt how to use them."

"But where did you get that gun? Did you bring it from America with you?"

Ginny looked down at the gun in her hand. She seemed surprised to see it. "This one? No. I found it. It was…. It was…. I remember! It was at the bottom of the fire escape. It was in a bag. I picked it up.

"But we are talking too much. I saw the men go down to the beach, but they will come back. So I think I must hurry. It would be a lot of trouble to kill them too, and I don't think I have enough bullets."

Stella was holding Jake's hand tightly and trying to think what to do.

*Keep her talking. Keep her talking. We need time.*

"Ginny!" said Stella. "Please tell us the rest of the story. Why was it a mistake to kill Wayne?"

"After Wayne left the boathouse, I heard a voice. It was Lou. He came out from behind the kayaks. He said, 'I see you found the extra gun I hid near the fire escape. I came in here to get the drugs. I heard Wayne open the door, so I hid. He was looking for something. I decided if he found the drugs, I would kill him. Thank you! You saved me the trouble. But it will be a big problem if he doesn't die.'

"Lou said Amy saw him moving the drugs from the beach to the boathouse. Amy told Lou that she wanted some of the drugs. She said if Lou didn't give her some, she would tell everyone. So Lou told her he would meet her on the balcony at two am and give her the drugs she wanted. Of course, he planned to kill her. Lou waited until Elsa was asleep. I made it easy for him because Amy and I had a big argument, and I went to sleep downstairs. Amy went out on the balcony to meet Lou and he killed her."

"So Lou killed Amy. Not Wayne. I'm sorry. But I don't know why Wayne was searching in the boatshed."

"He was looking for tools to fix the cell tower," said Delia.

"Oh," said Ginny. "I didn't know that."

"What happened next?" asked Stella.

"Well, I had a gun, and Lou had a gun. He was going to kill me, but I was very quick. I shot him while he was still talking. I always thought he talked too much," Ginny said dreamily.

Ginny looked half asleep. Her hand was not holding the gun tightly, and she was looking over their heads at the door.

*Maybe I can jump forward and take the gun,* thought Stella.

Stella must have moved a little, because Ginny suddenly looked very alert. She lifted the gun and pointed it at Stella. "I think I'll kill Delia first. Then you, Stella. I don't know about Jake. I don't know about Angela. It's too difficult. What do you think? I know I like Elsa and Chantelle. So I will kill them last."

## 21. POOR GINNY

The room was silent. Everyone was looking at Ginny as she pointed the gun at Delia. No one could breathe. Stella was still holding Jake's hand. *What does he understand? Does he know Ginny is going to kill me? Chris, I'm so sorry. I tried...*

Stella looked at Jake. He was looking past Ginny and out the window. Chris was looking in the window! *Oh Jake! Please! Don't say anything!*

"Sorry, Delia," said Ginny as she took aim to fire.

As Ginny fired the gun, Jake shouted "Chris!"

Ginny jumped in surprise, and the bullet missed Delia. At the same time, there was the sound of another shot and breaking glass. Ginny fell forward and the gun fell out of her hand.

Delia jumped up, and ran to Ginny. She put her fingers against her neck. "She's dead," she said. "Poor Ginny."

The next few minutes were chaotic. Chris ran into the room, followed by Gilbert and Max. Everyone was shouting, crying and hugging. Except Max. He was standing staring at Ginny. Stella left Chris hugging Jake, and went over to Max.

"Are you OK?" she asked.

"Poor Ginny," he said. "I didn't want to kill her."

"Oh Max. She was so sad about Amy. She lost her mind. She went crazy. She killed Wayne and Lou. She was going to kill Delia, then me, then Elsa and Chantelle. You saved us all! You mustn't feel bad."

Max sighed. He looked like a very old man. "I know. When we saw the boathouse door was open, we went in. We found Lou. He was dead. We knew that Ginny must have killed him. We guessed she killed him, because he had murdered Amy. There was a gun on the ground next to him. We thought that was the only gun. We hurried back here, and saw you all in the dining room. We couldn't hear anything, so we didn't know what to do. But when we saw that Ginny was going to shoot Delia, I had to act. I just wish it had been different."

When everything calmed down, Chris went to fix the cell tower. He took Jake with him. Max said he would call the police as soon as there was a signal.

Everyone else went to the guest lounge. Delia and Stella made hot drinks. They wrapped Elsa and Chantelle up in blankets. Angela went to the bar and came back with a bottle of whisky and glasses. She poured a drink for Gilbert and Max, and a much larger one for herself.

"I think you need this," she said. "I know I do."

Then to Stella's amazement, Angela sat down in front of the television and turned it on. "I hope Chris hurries with fixing that tower. I have missed a lot of television."

Stella looked at Delia. "Unbelievable!" laughed Delia, but Angela didn't hear her.

Stella's eyes closed. *I am so tired. I can't think anymore. She fell asleep.*

"Stella! Stella!" Chris was shaking her. "Wake up!"

Stella woke up and stared at Chris. "I'm sorry," he said. "You have had such a terrible time. I know you are very tired, but I need your help. The police helicopter will be here very soon. The police will ask to talk to everyone. It will take a long time. These people are our guests. We must look after them."

Stella stood up. She went to the kitchen and started to work. She took soup, bread, cheese and fruit to the guest lounge She made tea and coffee. She felt like a robot, but she thought if she didn't stop working, she would fall down and not get up again.

The police arrived. There were two helicopters. Then a boat arrived with more policemen. There were people everywhere. The police took charge of everything. Sometime after it was dark, a policeman came to the kitchen and asked Stella to come and talk to them.

Stella never remembered the rest of that night.

When she woke up the next morning, she was in her own

bedroom. The sun was shining through the window, and Chris was standing next to the bed with a cup of tea. He looked tired, but he was showered and dressed, and he was smiling.

"Jake?" said Stella. "Is he OK?"

"He's fine," said Chris. "The police won't let us go into the dining room or outside the front door. So Jake is on the balcony outside Chantelle's room. He has his PlayStation. He ate breakfast. He's happy. I don't know how much he remembers. Maybe everything. But we mustn't worry about that now."

He put the cup of tea down on the bedside table, sat down on the edge of the bed, and hugged her. "Oh Stella! You were in so much danger! You might have died!"

Stella felt stronger. "But Chris, I'm OK. Nothing bad happened to me. You and Jake are safe. But I'm thinking about Chantelle. She has no one. I love her. She is so brave. Can we ask her to stay with us?"

Chris kissed her. "Of course. If that is what you want. Now, drink your tea, take a shower and get dressed. We have another busy day."

All the policemen were very nice, but Stella found it difficult. No one could go to the dining room. No one could go outside. Delia and Gilbert spent the day in their bedroom. Max spent the day with the police. He didn't talk to anyone else. Angela was not allowed to go to the bedroom she had shared with Wayne, so she watched television and drank whisky all day.

Finally, the police took all the bodies away. Amy, Wayne, Lou and Ginny, thought Stella. Four people dead!

Later that night, everyone was asked to come to the guest lounge. The detective in charge of the enquiry spoke to them. "It's been very difficult for you all, but you did very well. Thank you.

"We will be here for a few days. But you are free to leave. Please tell me when you are leaving. Please give me your contact addresses before you go."

## 22. WHERE ARE YOU GOING?

The detective left the room. Max went with him. Stella looked at everyone who was left. *Our lives have changed forever,* she thought. *What happens now?*

Chris was talking. "If you want to go, I can take you to Walford in the motor launch. The police said it was OK. What do you want to do? Chantelle? Stella and I would like you to stay with us. For a little while, until you know what you want to do. Or forever, if you would like to?"

Chantelle jumped up from the sofa where she was sitting with Jake. She came to Stella and hugged her. "You have been so kind to me. I love you, and I love Jake. But I am going to live with Delia and Gilbert. But I will come back and visit you."

Stella hugged Chantelle back. Stella was crying. "I understand. I can make you smile, but Delia makes you laugh.

"Angela?" asked Chris. "What do you want to do? Do you want to leave now? Or do you want to stay for a while?"

Maybe for the first time, everyone was listening to Angela. "I answered Wayne's post on Tinder," she said. "I thought I was lonely, and I thought it would be nice to have company. But now I know I don't like company. I don't like partners or teenagers. I tried, but I like television better. I'm sorry Chantelle. I tried to like you, but I don't. I'll have a lot of money from Wayne, so I plan to enjoy myself."

"So," said Chris slowly. "You would like to leave here?"

"Yes," said Angela. "As soon as possible."

"Delia and I have been talking," said Gilbert. "We won the lottery. It was too much money for us. So many people came to us asking for money. We didn't know what to do. But now we know. Chantelle will come and live with us. We have no children, so Chantelle is a blessing. We will have a daughter!"

"We thought about everyone else," said Delia. "Elsa. What do you want to do?"

"I don't want to go back to working in the bar," said Elsa. "I was very stupid when I listened to Lou. If it's OK, I want to stay here."

Elsa looked at Stella. "You don't have to pay me. But I like it here. Can I stay for a while? Maybe I can help you?"

"Elsa," said Stella. "Four people died here. Do you think anyone will want to come to our hotel?"

"Why not?" Max was standing at the door of the lounge. "Nobody knows what happened here. The police don't want the newspapers or television to know. They want everything to be a secret. I think you can keep Blair House Hotel open."

## 23. A YEAR LATER

Stella is busy in the kitchen. She is preparing lunch for their guests. *We will be full,* she thinks. *Ten guests! No one ever found out what happened here. So people still think this is a good place to stay.*
*I think about Wayne, Amy and Ginny every day. I think about Lou too. What an evil man he was! But it's OK. Chantelle came to visit last week. She is so happy and relaxed. Her life with Gilbert and Delia is good.*
*Elsa lives with us now. She is dating Max. Maybe they will become a couple someday. But I hope she doesn't leave us too soon. I want her here when my baby is born. Chris and I told Jake. He is so happy that we will have a baby!*
*All of us who live here at Blair House remember what happened. But we still feel very lucky to live here.*

# THANK YOU

Thank you for reading Trapped. (Word count: 22,693) We hope you enjoyed the story.

If you would like to read more graded readers, please visit our website http://www.italkyoutalk.com

Other Level 4 graded readers include
Chi-obaa and Friends
Chi-obaa and Her Town
End House (Old Secrets – Modern Mysteries Book 1)
On the Run (Old Secrets – Modern Mysteries Book 3)
The Blue Lace Curtain (Old Secrets – Modern Mysteries Book 1)
The Box
The Legacy
The Witches of Nakashige
Vanished Away

# ABOUT THE AUTHOR

I Talk You Talk Press is a Japan-based publisher of language textbooks, graded readers and language learning/teaching resources.

Our team is made up of highly experienced language teachers and translators, who have all studied at least one additional language to an advanced level.

This experience enables us to design our materials from the perspective of both the teacher and the learner. We consult with both teachers and language learners when designing our textbooks and graded readers, and test our materials extensively in the classroom before publication.

We are a fast-growing press, and currently publish graded readers for learners of English. We publish new graded readers monthly.

www.ingramcontent.com/pod-product-compliance
Lightning Source LLC
Chambersburg PA
CBHW032210040426
42449CB00005B/530